THE IMPACT OF
CODY LEHE

JIM COOLEY

InspiringVoices·

Inspiring Voices books may be ordered through booksellers or by contacting:

Inspiring Voices
1663 Liberty Drive
Bloomington, IN 47403
www.inspiringvoices.com
1 (866) 697-5313

ISBN: 978-1-4624-1047-7 (sc)
ISBN: 978-1-4624-1048-4 (e)

Library of Congress Control Number: 2014950099

Printed in the United States of America.

Inspiring Voices rev. date: 9/11/2014

In honor of Cody Lehe, net proceeds from the sale of this book will help fund concussion education and research.

For Jean A. Cooley, who always encouraged me to keep writing.

"… I might have been given a bad break, but
I've got an awful lot to live for."

Lou Gehrig: July 4, 1939

CONTENTS

ACKNOWLEDGEMENTS

I would like to thank my mother for the inspiration to begin writing again. To my wife, Lisa, and my sons, Evan and Luke: thank you for the support and encouragement. Of course, I am grateful to the Lehe family for granting me access to their story. And lastly, "a whole heap of thanks" goes to Cody for allowing me to share in his journey.

Many people provided assistance throughout this process. I truly appreciate all of their efforts.

- Brent Fickle, Little Gridiron Coach, for his information about concussion awareness in youth football
- Brian Morris, M.D. who provided information regarding ImPACT testing
- Carol Bangert for her editorial assistance
- Christine Dahlenburg for the use of her professional photographs of Cody
- Connie Murray for her computer expertise.
- Corina Andersen, ATC, PTA, for her insights into recent changes in concussion management in the sport of football
- Eli Mansfield, friend of Cody, for information regarding the events related to Cody's injury
- Greg Martz, Cody's football coach at Frontier High School, who provided his perspective on Cody's injury
- Judi Brummett, for her ongoing email updates of Cody's early progress

- Mark Page, M.D., for reviewing medical information for accuracy
- Michelle and Joe Gerrety for early editorial suggestions
- Mike DeBoy, IHSAA football referee, for his perspective on concussion awareness
- Neil Bullock, for sharing his concussion experience
- The Purdue Neurotrauma Group: Larry Leverenz, Ph.D., Eric Nauman, Ph.D., and Thomas Talavage, Ph.D, for sharing their research and expert opinions on the subject of concussions
- The B.E.S.T. Book Club for final editing review
- Tracy Cooley for providing marketing suggestions

PREFACE

My mother always wanted me to be a writer. In fourth grade, I won an award for a paper I had written about Patrick Henry. I vividly remember how pleased my mom looked, as she sat in the front row of a meeting of the Daughters of the American Revolution, while I read my story. Mom had big plans for me. She thought I might aspire to become a sports reporter, as it would combine my love of sports and my affinity towards writing. My mother was used to getting her way. I won't say that she was disappointed when I pursued a career in physical therapy, but she always wanted me to keep writing.

She was pleased when I took a six-month sabbatical from my job to travel to Oregon and try my hand at writing children's stories. There, I wrote a lot and did just as much hiking. When I finished a story, I would mail it to my mother for her review. Unfortunately, she liked my writing much more than the publishing houses did.

So, I returned to my job, married, and soon had two sons. I would still write occasionally, but the business of raising two young boys cut into any time I could devote to writing. Whatever I did complete, I would pass along to my mother, who always was full of praise and suggestions.

I wrote my final story more than five years ago. It was a children's picture book about a grandmother who loved to celebrate Easter. Her favorite part was the Easter Treasure Hunt. And, it was her grandsons' favorite, as well. The grandma would put rhyming clues onto egg-shaped colored paper, so that a series would direct her grandchildren on a quest to locate their Easter baskets. The boys loved to find their hidden treasures of chocolate bunnies, hand-dipped candies, colored eggs, and kites.

"Hop like a bunny, my little one.

Go peek at the water spigot.

Hurry now, run, run, run."

The grandsons would rush to find the next clue. After four or five such searches, they'd be directed to their treasure. The boys would delight in their goodies, and then scramble to search for the second brother's basket.

And, so it went, Easter after Easter, as the boys grew older. Their father enjoyed each Easter Treasure Hunt as much as his sons did, reliving the joy of past Easters of his youth. One year, though, the grandmother began to feel weak. When Easter arrived, she did not have the energy to make the clues for her grandchildren.

Knowing that Grandma did not feel well, the boys were saddened by the thought of missing their Easter tradition. So, they made an Easter hunt for their grandmother. They placed clues in a small area of the house, so that their grandmother would not have to walk far. They even made her a special surprise for the end of the search.

I elaborated on this story for my mother in April 2008, two weeks after she had been diagnosed with stage IV colon cancer. Her grandsons illustrated the tale. When my parents came to our house to celebrate Easter, we read her the story. Then, we all helped her search for her Easter surprise. We laughed; I cried, and my mother shook her head and told me not to be such a baby.

That was Mom's final Easter. She passed away in August of that year. I didn't feel like writing anymore, until now. Truthfully, the normal trappings of everyday life, along with coaching my sons' sports teams, left little time to sit and write. Besides, my biggest literary fan was no longer present to read what I might have composed, anyway.

And so, a busy life moved forward. I had just finished coaching my son's elementary school basketball team and was looking forward to a Sunday when we had no AAU basketball games. There was no travel baseball practice until that evening, and soccer season would not start for two more weeks. The boys had spent the night at their friend's house, and we had all gone to church on Saturday evening. My wife and I were looking forward to sleeping late.

However at 4:30 a.m., I awoke with the story that will follow, in my mind. I hadn't thought of Cody Lehe, the subject of this story, since I had seen him for a physical therapy session, the previous Thursday afternoon. Yet, on the morning of March 7, 2010, I could not get Cody out of my mind. I rolled over and tried to go back to sleep, but as I lay there I kept thinking about Cody and his recent past. As my mind drifted in and out of sleep, I imagined a story about Cody's life. It was a very vivid tale, not simply a passage or two, but an outline of each chapter, laid out before me.

I eventually gave up on sleep and climbed from bed. I wandered into our office, and began to type. That is where my wife found me three hours later, still typing. Looking up from the computer, I told her how I had been awakened with the story stuck in my mind.

"That was your mother that woke you up," my wife chuckled. "She's up in heaven inspiring you. She wanted you to get up, and get busy writing."

"You might be right," I laughed. "But couldn't she have waited until 7 o'clock?"

And, so I have written. Sometimes I felt inspired, sometimes not so much. Yet, no matter what, it felt good to write again. Through my writing, I have laughed and cried as I delved into Cody's story. I hope that you find it as moving as I have. I think that my mom would have enjoyed it.

Jim Cooley
December 2013

INTRODUCTION

My name is Jim Cooley and I have been a physical therapist for 20 years. For 15 of those years, I have been performing home visits for First Steps, an early intervention program in the state of Indiana. In addition to outpatient and school-based physical therapy, I also do some homebound services for students who are unable to attend school due to health or physical challenges. In my job, I am afforded a glimpse into the daily lives of the families and children for whom I provide services. Initially, most are on their best, guarded behavior. But as I visit week after week, I become woven into the fabric of the family's daily life. While I work with the child on developmental activities, family life tends to unfold around me.

I have been treated to a 30-year-old dad singing karaoke to AC/DC's "Shook Me All Night Long," while his wife sat beside me on the floor playing with their son, as if there were nothing abnormal about the situation. On another home visit, I was told by police to stand with my hands raised, while they entered with a warrant, to search the apartment for drugs. I have sadly watched as parents who were trying to do their best for their ill child, slowly began to no longer be able to support one another in this challenging struggle. And, I cried as I left the house of a child who had succumbed to seizure and breathing difficulties. This was something the parents knew was inevitable, but it was just as painful as if it had been unexpected.

However, no family has touched me like the one that will be described in the following pages. Perhaps it is the patient himself. Cody Lehe is a hilarious and uplifting young man. Sometimes the hour that I spend in physical therapy with a patient can move so slowly, that I swear that my watch has stopped. That is not the case at Cody's house. Cody is a pleasant and hard-working young man with a contagious laugh.

Perhaps my affinity grows from my own two sons, whom I can see in Cody. I find myself praying that my sons develop into the fine young man that Cody has become. But, that affinity is most likely due to the hope that flows from the Lehe household. There could be overwhelming anger about the severe brain injury that Cody incurred while playing football. Yet, I have never sensed despair in the Lehe family. I am sure they have dealt with the anger and resentment that must surround Cody's injury, but it has never manifested itself during my many visits.

The story that follows was written over a span of four years. It covers Cody's recovery and rehabilitation from 2006 through 2014. I began writing about the entertaining aspects of Cody's therapy sessions in March 2010. This compilation continued over the next year and a half. Cody's story then lay dormant over the next two years, until once again I received the motivation to complete the research portion of this novel. (Please bear with the time-frame of this story. Most of my interactions with Cody are quoted in present tense, even though some of those words were spoken over three years ago. I decided it would be more confusing to transition between past and present tense.)

The purpose of <u>The Impact of Cody Lehe</u> is not to turn anyone away from the sport of football. That is not what Cody would want. Rather, the goal of this story is to provide a perspective to young athletes facing the symptoms of a concussion. In the pages that follow, I will share a glimpse into Cody's life with you. His life has inspired me on many levels, and my hope is I can write well enough to inspire you, as well.

It should be noted that physical therapists, as all medical personnel, take patient privacy very seriously. Information about Cody, shared in this story, is provided to help increase awareness surrounding concussions. This information is being shared with the blessing of Cody and his family.

CHAPTER 1

THE INJURY

In some areas of the United States there are spectacular vistas that await you as your car makes a turn along your commute. In Oregon and Colorado the Cascade and Rocky mountain ranges provide inspiration, as you see the far-off peaks that appear close enough to touch. That's not the case in Indiana, where there is little to block your view. On clear days, one can see for miles, with only a grain silo or telephone pole obscuring the horizon. That has changed, in certain areas, over the past few years. Wind turbines now dominate the skyline in portions of White County. These 400-foot tall creatures reach toward the heavens, in an otherwise flat and open countryside. The turbines have been erected in long lines scattered around Brookston and Chalmers, and one cannot help but watch as they make their constant, rhythmic turns.

But in the fall of 2006, the turbines had not yet made their way to Indiana. For players on the Falcon Football Field, there was nothing on the horizon to distract them from their task. No turning of the wind turbine blades would take away from the players' intensity as they prepared for their upcoming sectional game against Pioneer. Frontier had won its opening round sectional game and had been rewarded with no practice on Monday. Tuesday's practice was a light one, to keep everyone healthy going into the big game on Friday.

At practice, players were to go approximately 75 percent, as they walked through the plays. The defense lined up opposite their offensive teammates. Instead of making tackles, players were to "pop pads", but

1

have no real hits. Cody, a starter on offense and defense, was especially glad to be participating in practice today, as he had just been cleared to play in the upcoming game. In the sectional game that previous week, a win against Caston High School, Cody had suffered a concussion.

In that game on Friday October 20, 2006, Cody had led his team onto the field. As a senior, Cody had earned the position of a team captain. He had played varsity since his freshman year. He was now a linebacker on defense and played center on offense. With a limited number of players on the team, many of the stronger members played on both sides of the ball. This was challenging – especially when the opposing offense had time to rest when its defense was on the field. But, Cody relished the challenge, and entering the sectional game, he had helped lead the team to a 6-4 record. Coach Greg Martz knew that Cody was a key member of his team.

"Every time I needed something from a leadership perspective, Cody is who I would look to," Martz says.

As he ran onto the field, Cody proudly displayed his black, number 55 jersey. He vowed that this would not be his final time to wear the Frontier uniform. The Falcons were playing the Caston High School Comets in the first round of sectionals. (This state tournament would crown the Class A Indiana State Football Champions.) The Falcons played a terrific first half of football, and were riding high as they entered the locker room at half time.

Mid-way through the second half, Cody lined up with the punt return team. The ball sailed over his head. During punt and kick-off returns, the defensive players run full speed in an effort to break through the line to make a tackle. Since Frontier was receiving the ball, Cody's job was to block for his punt returner in an effort to keep the tacklers at bay. The defensive player in Cody's lane barreled toward him, and as he had done hundreds of times before, Cody ran full-out toward his assignment. As Cody lowered his head to make the block, the defensive player lowered his helmet, as well.

It was a vicious impact, helmet to helmet, but both players jumped to their feet to show that neither had been hurt. Cody was checked out by the coaching staff, on the sideline. Teammates report that Cody experienced some dizziness and vision difficulties, but number 55 insisted he was fine.

Cody missed only a few plays before returning. The Falcons ended up with a 22-0 win. After the game, the Frontier coaching staff spoke with the Lehes. The coaches indicated that Cody had taken a good hit, but that he seemed to be doing fine. They encouraged the Lehes to keep an eye on Cody over the weekend, and to check him every few hours to make sure he was able to respond normally.

That evening, Cody enjoyed watching the high school football highlight show on local television, but he could only do so by looking sideways through a slit in his fingers. He could not look directly at the bright light of the television. Even then, he could only look for short intervals before having to turn away. This caused Cody's mother, Becky, some concern. After he went to bed, Becky checked on Cody every few hours through the night, waking him up to make sure he was responsive.

On Saturday morning, Cody appeared to be fine. Coach Martz had the team watch game films, but otherwise the players were given the weekend to recuperate before beginning practice to prepare for the upcoming game against Pioneer. By Saturday afternoon, Cody assured his mother that he was doing better. He went to a tailgate party for a Purdue University football game that afternoon, and made a college visit with his girlfriend on Sunday. Nevertheless, Cody's headache, secretly, still lingered, a reminder of the hit that he had taken and inflicted on the football field.

On Tuesday morning, Becky received a phone call from school. Cody had called to report his headache to her. "I really need to see a doctor," he told his mother. Cody was not one to complain, especially when it came to sports, so Becky took him to the emergency room at Lafayette Home Hospital.

Cody was seen by a physician who took his complaints seriously. The doctor checked Cody's pupil dilation and his response to simple questions, but Cody was not experiencing these symptoms. He displayed no nausea or confusion. Cody's only symptom was a headache. The doctor ordered a CT (computerized tomography) scan that morning. The results were normal. Cody's brain showed no signs of injury. That was all Cody needed to hear.

The physician encouraged Cody not to play football if his headaches persisted, but in the mind of an 18-year-old, a clean CT scan was all he needed in order to return to the field. Having participated in the sport of football since age 10, Cody had played with a variety of lingering injuries. This was no different, he thought.

Coach Martz was aware of Cody's E.R. visit by the time the senior had returned to school. "I made it a point to check in with Cody," (to see how he was feeling) the coach says.

On the practice field, during stretches, he again asked Cody how he was doing. Each time, Cody replied with the answer that would allow him to play on Friday.

The Falcons were playing Pioneer in a second round game of sectionals, and Cody did not want to miss the opportunity to help lead his team to victory. The Falcons had not won a sectional championship since 1991. Cody wanted to be a member of the next team to be crowned sectional champions. And, he would not miss a practice for something as simple as a headache that had already been checked out.

Eli Mansfield, put it this way, (there was) "never a time that I can remember that Cody didn't give 100 percent. He was full go all the time; that's just the way Cody was."

Looking back, Coach Martz says, "I wish Cody would have told one of the coaches. We really didn't know that he still had a headache. We would have done the right thing and sat him out. But, Cody probably knew that we would sit him out, and that is why he didn't say anything."

There was nothing extraordinary about the collision between Cody and an offensive player, early in the practice on Tuesday October 24, 2006. However, the result of this minor impact was immense. The ball carrier tossed the ball back to the coach, as the team lined up for the next series of plays. Shortly thereafter, the team broke for a water break.

While walking to the sideline, Cody grabbed the back of a teammate's jersey then lowered himself to the ground.

Friend and teammate, Eli Mansfield saw Cody go down on one knee then fall to the turf.

"I hurried over to Cody," recalls Eli, "but none of us really knew what to do. The coaches ran over to check on Cody. We all knew it was pretty serious."

Frontier High School is in the town of Chalmers, Indiana, population 508. The school serves students in the southwest portion of White County, and its enrollment nears 240 students, in its four grades. An athletic trainer is present at games and some practices for this small school, but cannot be at every practice. So, Coach Greg Martz ran to where his star player lay on the ground.

"Next thing I knew, Cody had collapsed," recalls Coach Martz. "I remember it as crystal clear as the day it happened."

At 3:45p.m., on Tuesday October 24th, four days after his initial concussion, Cody's parents received a phone call from the school, asking them to come immediately, as Cody had been injured.

"I expected Cody to be sitting there rolling his eyes when I arrived, asking why in the world they had to call me," says Becky. But, when Dale and Becky Lehe pulled up to Falcon Field, Cody was not sitting up. He was initially unresponsive. This had progressed to seizure activity.

Fortunately, one of the assistant coaches was also an EMT. He took over immediately and cared for Cody until the ambulance arrived. Once it did, Cody was rushed back to Home Hospital, where another CT scan was completed. This time, the scan revealed horrific damage. Cody was flown by helicopter to Methodist Hospital, where he remained comatose.

CHAPTER 2

TRAUMA TO THE BRAIN

If you were to see Cody (while he was sitting down) today, initially there would be little to distinguish his injury. The only outward remnant is the large scar at the base of his throat. This is a reminder of the tracheostomy that remained in place for over three months, as a ventilator helped Cody to breathe. Cody is tall, at six feet two inches, but he cannot stand without support. Cody does rely on his manual wheelchair to get around, but will utilize a power scooter when he wants to maneuver more quickly. Cody has brown hair and brown eyes with a mischievous glint.

Once you meet Cody, the first thing that would strike you is his energetic and outgoing personality. He is quick to laugh and to share a smile. The young man is genuinely happy to meet a new friend or speak with an old one. Cody always has a humorous response to your conversation and is an excellent audience for a joke. Even a not-so-funny attempt at humor generally receives a raucous response of laughter. Any struggling comic would be glad to find Cody in the front row of his or her show. Cody's laughter comes easily and is contagious.

After speaking with Cody for a short while, one might find some of his mannerisms a bit odd. He frequently cocks his head to one side and sits with arms outstretched as he awaits your response. While Cody is quick-witted in his responses, he may not have an easy reply to a simple question about his day. Cody frequently cannot recall what has recently taken place, and he will typically need to check with his mother to provide an answer.

Cody's short-term memory has been impacted by his injury, and he could not tell you, without prompting, if he went to a basketball game the previous evening or what he had for breakfast. If Cody were to hear a new or unusual word during your conversation, he may ask you to please spell it. Aside from these few oddities, a person would find themselves leaving a conversation with Cody entertained and engaged by a delightful, sincere, young man.

This was not the case for more than a year after Cody's injury. Even following his arousal from coma, Cody's recovery was slow and uncertain. Cody sustained an injury called Second-Impact Syndrome. It is the result of a blow (or an even less traumatic event) to the head, before the brain's recovery from an earlier injury is complete. In Cody's case, he was still recovering from the concussion he sustained in the game against Caston, when he suffered another injury at practice a few days later. The chance of survival for those diagnosed with Second-Impact Syndrome is only about 50 percent. This diagnosis is rare, affecting only a handful of high school and college athletes each year.

The diagnosis of traumatic brain injury is not rare. A traumatic brain injury (TBI) is caused by a knock or bump to the head that disrupts brain function. The term "concussion" is sometimes used interchangeably with a mild TBI. Technically, a concussion should be considered a subset of a mild traumatic brain injury. Concussions have been referred to as a "ding" or "bell-ringer". These terms sound innocuous, likely referring to the fuzzy sounds one sometimes hears after being struck in the head. The term traumatic brain injury sounds much more serious, and accurately describes this event.

One can sustain a blow to the head without having it considered a TBI. However, if there is a brief change in mental status or a loss of consciousness, a brain injury is said to have occurred. These brief changes are classified as a mild brain injury. In Cody's case, his first injury was a mild traumatic brain injury, his second was severe. A severe traumatic brain injury is determined by an extended period of unconsciousness or amnesia after the injury. The Brain Injury Association of America indicates that every 15 to 20 seconds, someone sustains a brain injury.[1] The majority of these individuals suffer a mild TBI, which despite its designation, can be significant in challenges to long-term memory, problem solving, and other areas.

As part of my physical therapy training, I completed four clinical affiliations. These unpaid internships are similar to student teaching rotations for those majoring in education. Three of my rotations were in the state of Indiana, but I was lucky enough to travel to Denver, Colorado for my final affiliation. In addition to hiking, skiing, and mountain biking, I gained valuable experience at Spalding Rehabilitation Center. During my rotation in this neurological rehabilitation setting, I was able to work with patients diagnosed with multiple sclerosis, cerebrovascular accident (stroke), and other neurological injuries.

While there, I was able to spend a morning in the adjacent Craig Hospital Rehabilitation Unit. There, patients requiring longer-term and more specialized care were seen for a variety of therapies. Craig Hospital specializes in the treatment of patients with the diagnoses of spinal cord injury and traumatic brain injury.

Many of the patients had been injured in such pursuits as rock climbing, motocross sports, skiing accidents, or diving injuries. Others were rehabilitating from car accidents. The majority of patients that I met on this busy unit were 16-24 year-old males. They were all struggling to learn to live with their new physical (and sometimes cognitive) limitations, including, for many, how to rely on a wheelchair for mobility.

According to the Centers for Disease Control, each year in the United States, 52,000 deaths and 275,000 hospitalizations occur as a result of traumatic brain injury. Some 1.365 million people seek hospital treatment and are released after a TBI.[2] In the majority of the cases where a person is released, the diagnosis is a concussion. A concussion is not usually life threatening, but can have long-term effects upon a person's physical, psychological, and cognitive function.

Fifteen- to 19 year-olds are at the greatest risk for sustaining a brain injury, with males being nearly twice as likely to be involved in such an accident as girls. Activities such as diving into shallow pools, riding ATV's in a reckless manner, and driving a car at high speeds, put teenage boys at a higher risk. The leading causes of a TBI are vehicular accidents (car, motorcycle, ATV, boat, and bicycle) accounting for more than 50 percent of the cases. Assaults, falls, sports-related injuries, and attempted suicides account for the rest. Recently, the cases of active military personnel sustaining TBIs have increased dramatically. The IEDs (improvised explosive devices or roadside bombs) being used in warfare in Iraq and Afghanistan have resulted in this dreadful increase.

Cody fits into the age group at greatest risk, but he was not participating in what would be considered a particularly high-risk activity. However, sports and recreation-related accidents account for a significant portion of youth injuries. Most people are aware of the injuries that occur in high-contact sports, such as football. Many have watched the replays of a star quarterback or running back, whose leg is twisted under him in an unnatural position. We might say a prayer when a player takes a vicious hit and must be carted off the field with a neck brace attached as a preventive measure.

However, until recently concussions and brain injuries were not viewed with the seriousness of other more visible injuries. Troy Aikman, retired Dallas Cowboys quarterback and now an NFL announcer, is one of the first football players that I recall who suffered numerous, documented concussions during his playing career. Aikman was selected to the Pro Bowl six times, and was a three-time Super Bowl champion. However, he later indicated that he does not remember playing in the 1993 NFC Championship game against San Francisco.[3] Aikman's injuries led to his early retirement after the 2000 season.

Near the end of the 2009 football season, teammates questioned the commitment of Pittsburgh Steelers quarterback Ben Roethlisberger after he sat out a second consecutive game -- which likely was a major cause of the team missing the play-offs -- due to concerns surrounding a concussion. Roethlisberger's teammates pointed out that he looked fine and was able to take snaps in practice and wondered why he could not play. Those same teammates likely would not have questioned their quarterback's courage, if he had been hobbling around at practice during the week, secondary to knee pain, or had been receiving therapy for a more physically evident injury. However, a concussion does not present with outward symptoms immediately noticeable by others. This makes it difficult to detect.

The NFL has adopted a policy where teammates are encouraged to notify a coach if another player is acting abnormally at practice or in the locker room, after sustaining a blow to the head. Each team has a representative who is responsible for monitoring players who have sustained a hit during a game. However, in a sport where players constantly are taking blows, it is difficult to determine, when one particular hit may be consequential. Additionally, in a league where players often reach their position by being tough enough to battle through injury, some may not want to be perceived as weak, or risk a chance of someone taking their position.

As in the NFL, a tough football mentality filters down through each level of the sport. As the great Green Bay Packers coach Vince Lombardi, once said: "Football is not a contact sport, it's a collision sport – dancing is a contact sport."[4]

As Lombardi notes, football is not a game for the meek. This is not to say that other sports do not carry the risk for head injury. In fact, while football has a high incidence of mild traumatic brain injury, other sports, such as soccer (heading the ball), baseball (being hit by a pitch or running into the wall while catching the ball in the outfield), and basketball (hitting the floor after a rebound or bumping heads with another player) all present opportunities for injury. Protective gear is present in some sports, while not a necessity in others.

In an October 2013 report, the National Academy of Sciences found that high school football players do, in fact, present with the highest rate of concussion incidence (11.2 for every 10,000 "athletic exposures"). Other high school sports had significant incidences, as well, with boys lacrosse at 6.9/ 10,000, girls soccer at 6.7, and wrestling at 6.2.[5] According to the Centers for Disease Control, in the United States an estimated 173,285 sports-related traumatic brain injuries are treated each year in emergency rooms.[6] The National Academy of Sciences found that concussive events in youth, under 19 years of age, nearly doubled in reported cases from 2001 to 2009.[7] It is suspected that up to twice as many concussions go unreported.

In his study, Michael McCrea, Ph.D., of the Neurosciences Center, Waukesha Memorial Hospital, looked at 1,631 football players from 15 U.S. colleges, from 1999 to 2001. Ninety-four players were diagnosed as suffering from a concussion, based on the American Academy of Neurology criteria. The researchers assessed these players who experienced a concussion at 3, 5, 7, and 90 days after injury. On average, cognitive functioning symptoms (short-term memory) improved to baseline levels within 5 to 7 days. Balance deficits improved within 3-5 days. Those with repeat concussions likely sustained them within the first few weeks after the initial injury, and the subsequent concussion presented with increased symptoms as compared to the first.[8]

In an editorial response to the aforementioned study, Douglas McKeag, M.D.,M.S., of the Indiana School of Medicine, suggested that any athlete with a concussion be removed from the activity. He or she should not be allowed to return to the activity until his or her symptoms completely resolve. Any athlete with a prolonged loss of consciousness or evidence of amnesia should not be allowed to return to the sport that same day. He also suggested that trained personnel should perform the careful and repeated assessment following any concussive event, and lastly, that any patient with symptoms that spiral downward be referred to a specialist for consultation. Athletes with a cumulative history of head trauma should be informed about the risk of repeat concussions before continuing to play contact sports.[9]

In these 2003 articles, a shift had begun to occur from defining a concussion as a loss of consciousness. Rather, a movement began toward understanding concussions as an alteration in consciousness. Most data support the fact that only 10 percent of diagnosed concussions result in a loss of consciousness. Over the past 10 years, a shift has occurred in the understanding of the dangers of continued activity with a concussion. Any athlete that is suspected of a concussion should be removed from play. A report by the American Medical Society for Sports Medicine regarding best practices for concussion management notes that concussions are typically self-limiting. However, the report goes on to emphasize that studies have shown that when activity resumes before the brain has fully recovered from a concussive event, the brain may be vulnerable to prolonged or more severe dysfunction.[10]

And while the National Football League has made headlines with concerns regarding concussion awareness and the long-term effects of head impacts on its players, there are equal concerns regarding concussions in youth sports. In 2014, the National Academy of Sciences issued an alarming report that found high school football players suffer concussions at nearly twice the rate of college players.[11] Additionally, the Centers for Disease Control indicate that 65 percent of concussions occur in youth, age 5 to 18.[12]

There are several reasons for this. First, more children are active in sports and other activities that might lead to concussions, compared to more sedentary adults. Second, from a medical standpoint, there is the concern that a younger brain is still developing and thus more susceptible to injury. In children and adolescents, axons are less myelinated (insulating layer of nerves) and dura (protective layer of the brain) is not as well developed, so that these areas are more at risk, in cases of impact. Finally, the neck musculature of children and teens is not as well developed as in adults. Thus, impacts have greater repercussions in youth secondary to less stabilization via the muscles of the neck.

§§ §§ §§ §§ §§ §§ §§ §§ §§ §§ §§ §§ §§ §§

Cody cannot recall what he felt like after being struck on the football field. His mother is only aware of his complaints of a headache after his first injury. We have all likely experienced moments of feeling stunned after striking our head on a table or countertop after picking an item from the floor. Neil Bullock, a 1987 Indiana All-State selection at wide receiver who went on to play football in junior college, does recall his experience with a concussion. It happened during a football game in high school. He does not remember the hit.

"The first thing I recall," explains Bullock, "was waking up on the ground. I was lying on my back and people were gathered around me. My vision was fuzzy and I could not hear anything. I knew that people were talking, because their mouths were moving. Everything was moving in slow motion. After about 10 seconds things began to clear. It was like coming out of a tunnel. I could hear more, but only gradually, until things went back to normal."

Bullock's perspective is valuable, but as previously noted, only a small percentage of concussions result in such a loss of consciousness. Others, who suffer a head trauma, may experience a challenge to think clearly. New Orleans Saints quarterback Drew Brees describes such an incident in his book, Coming Back Stronger.

> *"It was an all-out blitz. John McGraw and Jonathon Vilma came untouched up the middle, and after I let go of the ball, they each took turns hitting me in the head like a pinball machine. Then my head smacked the ground. The first thing I remember after my vision cleared was staring at the ground and seeing everything spinning. I spat what felt like gravel out of my mouth. Three of my teeth were chipped. At that point, I didn't know I had a concussion, so I stayed in the game. The play came in my headset, but I could barely comprehend the words. I felt like I was underwater. I handed off to LaDamian Tomlinson, and he went in for a touchdown. We celebrated, but I was out of it. I almost ran to the wrong sideline.*
>
> *By the time I reached our sideline, everything was spinning. The doctors came over to look at me and did the normal routine for a potential head injury. They said three unrelated words — something like 'Dog, Banana, Bicycle'.*

Then they asked me how I felt and checked me out. A couple of minutes later they asked, 'What were those three words we said to you earlier?'

What are you talking about?' I said.

At that point, they knew there was a problem."[13]

Brees came out of that game, despite his protests. The coaches and medical personnel were aware of the seriousness of such a head injury. His story gives us an insight into what athletes may experience following a concussive event.

At the time of Cody's injury, concussions were typically classified in three grades. Grade 1 had symptoms of confusion and poor concentration, which resolved within 15 minutes. No loss of consciousness occurred. The recommendations were for the player to be removed from the game, with immediate examination and at consistent 5-minute intervals until he or she improved. The player was allowed to return to the game if symptoms resolved within this timeframe.

Grade 2 concussions were classified with similar criteria, but with symptoms lasting longer than 15 minutes. The player was removed from the game and could not return that same day. A second Grade 2 concussion would limit a player from returning for at least two weeks after symptoms improved.

Lastly, Grade 3 concussions occurred when there was any (even for seconds) loss of consciousness. That player was recommended to be taken to the emergency room, with an immediate neurological examination. That exam was recommended for follow-up at daily intervals. The player with a Grade 3 concussion was not allowed to return to play for at least one week after symptoms had cleared, if they suffered a brief (seconds) loss of consciousness. If that loss of consciousness lasted for minutes, the player should not return for two weeks after symptoms had cleared. Athletes with a second Grade 3 concussion could not return for at least one month.[14]

While this method for grading concussions is no longer utilized, this system does provide us with some insight into how athletes were held from and brought back to sporting activities, as recently as seven years ago. Today, concussions are examined on an individual basis. Rather than applying grades to a concussion, Dr. Brian Morris, of Franciscan Alliance in Lafayette, Indiana, who is board certified in sports medicine, looks at concussions in regards to length of recovery. Morris administers the ImPACT (Immediate Post-Concussion Assessment and Cognitive Testing) Test to athletes. This allows the athlete to return to action based on meeting certain pre-established criteria in response to computer-administered testing. This form of neurocognitive testing is not utilized in isolation. Clinical judgment, subjective information from the athlete, and other tools (such as balance testing) are all considered in a thorough concussion assessment.

Think of the brain as a gelatinous mass that is surrounded by shock absorbing fluid (cerebrospinal fluid), wrapped in a protective membrane (meninges), all protected by a hard outer layer (the skull). This all works pretty well for the typical bruises and bumps of life. However, these protective mechanisms cannot withstand those moments of high impacts. In some accidents, the brain is damaged when the head moves forward, striking a stationary object. In others, the brain is damaged when the head is struck by a moving object. In football both scenarios, or a combination of the two, can occur. A player can be slammed to the ground during a tackle, striking his head against the static, hard surface. On other occasions, the player can take a blow to the head, when he is struck by a fast moving tackler (or as the tackler himself).

In a variety of sporting activities, these blows can be substantial. In their ongoing research measuring impacts with helmet accelerometers, the Purdue Neurotrauma Group has recorded impacts up to 289 Gs.[15] G refers to the force of acceleration due to gravity. An object moves at 3 Gs, if its motion is three times the force of gravity. Rollercoaster riders, for example, experience 3 Gs of force. A hit of nearly 300 Gs in football is extreme, but those measuring greater than 100 Gs are not uncommon. Comparatively, a soccer player heading a ball can experience an impact of 20 Gs.

These events can have a horrible effect on the well-protected, but relatively delicate master controller of the body -- the brain. The brain is primarily composed of a network of nerve cells. Neurons do the much of the work of this system. They help direct bodily activities such as movement and digestion, while accounting for the more diverse work of problem solving and personality. These diverse neurons communicate with one another, along with other parts of the body, through connections called axons. These transmission lines can run long distances through the brain and often wind together.

When a strong blow to the head occurs, two types of damage can result. First, there is the blunt force at the point of impact, which can cause damage to that specific area. Frequently, as the brain slides forward resulting in this impact, it will strike, then bounce back to hit the opposite side of the skull. This results in damage on the opposite side of the initial impact. Additionally, if twisting takes place during the accident, a shearing effect can occur, where the axons can be ripped in two, causing connections between neurons to be severed. In this hurricane of events that takes place within the skull, a variety of injuries can occur, with diffuse results.

Concussions upset the balance of ions and metabolism in the brain. Increased energy is required for the brain to heal itself from a concussion. The challenge lies in the fact that decreased blood flow and reduced energy production, in injured areas, limit this process. It takes time for the brain to heal. If the brain is not granted rest and time to recuperate, it is at risk for further injury.

Figure 1 (in the image and photo insert located in the center of this book) shows a cross-section of a brain. You can see how the base of the brain (brainstem and cerebellum) are tightly packed in the posterior fossa of the skull. Typically, little damage occurs in this area, unless swelling causes a herniation of this region. (Swelling or edema can be especially problematic in the brain, as there is only so much space for the swelling to go in the tightly packed shell.) Sitting on this stalk of medulla, is 3 ½ pounds of soft matter. There is greater room for shifting and movement in this upper portion of the brain, and hence, where most damage occurs in a typical concussion.

The outcomes for those suffering from a head trauma depend on the type of injury. There are stories of people who have sustained an open head wound (such as from a gun shot) who have made miraculous improvements. If no major blood vessels are struck and if no infection results, these individuals may be able to make a full recovery. The brain is remarkably adaptable, and can replace some of the connections lost in a single injury. In open head wounds, damage typically is isolated to specific regions of the brain. However, in a severe closed head injury, the areas of damage are so great and so diffuse, that the brain often cannot fully accommodate these areas of injury. The brain is quite resilient, but only to a point.

CHAPTER 3

THE DECISION

Several tornadoes blew through mid-north Indiana on a Sunday in November 2013. The following day, I traveled between Frontier Elementary School and Tri-County High School, surveying the damage along the way. There was a long stretch of county road that appeared somewhat barren, with the fields of corn and soybeans being recently harvested. There were only a few houses and buildings along my route, but most had experienced damage. The tin roofs of several hog barns had blown across the road, with pieces strewn throughout the field. The augers of five grain bins had been knocked down. They lay twisted amidst the sad landscape of the surrounding farm.

One building from that drive stands out in my memory. A barn with a tin roof sustained much damage, but the sheets of metal were still attached. The inner rafters and beams of the roof were exposed, and work would need to be done quickly to nail the roof back down and replace damaged pieces. But, with quick action, the barn would be stable again and ready to face the impending winter.

I imagine that Cody's brain, after his first concussion, was similar to this damaged barn. After the Caston game, Cody's brain was injured. The headaches and sensitivity to light were signs of this damage. As for the farmer with the barn, if another storm came along before the roof was repaired, the rest of the roof would likely be destroyed. For Cody, another storm did come along, a result of the light hit in practice -- even so slight, it set off a cascade of events that changed Cody's life forever.

55   55   55   55   55   55   55   55   55   55   55   55   55   55

It was my freshman year of college, and a large amount of snow had fallen while we sat inside the chapel for a Christmas service. When we walked outside, people were giddily making snow balls and frolicking in the fluffy precipitation. As a car drove slowly past the chapel, my friend Bob, grabbed hold of the bumper and squatted as he slid on his feet for more than 100 feet behind the vehicle.

When I caught up to him, I asked, "What in the world were you doing?"

"Bumper sliding," he said grinning. "I used to do it after every snow with my buddies during high school."

When another friend drove by, we flagged him down. Both Bob and I grabbed hold of the bumper to slide along, back to our dorm. When we returned to school in the second semester, we went bumper sliding (or hitching, as other friends called it) after nearly every snow. We even had contests to see who was the most brave (or most stupid) bumper slider. In these contests, bumper sliders reached speeds of more than 30 miles an hour.

I recount this story for a reason. Sometimes young adults don't make sound decisions. I now shudder to think about what could have gone wrong if a car would have stopped suddenly and one of us ended up under a tire. But, at the time, I did not consider the dangers involved. Teens and young adults, especially boys, often see themselves as invincible. They may not look toward the future and what effect their actions might have.

If Cody could have known the dangers that he faced by returning too quickly to the football field, he would not have chosen to put on his helmet that fourth week of October 2006. As Cody squinted and turned away while viewing television after the Caston game, he had to know that something was quite wrong. The headaches that lingered, which sent him to the emergency room, were an indication that his brain needed time to heal.

Eli Mansfield, Cody's teammate and friend, was later inspired by Cody to enter sports medicine. With an athletic training background, Eli looks back at Cody's initial injury. Eli recalls Cody seeming a little fuzzy for a couple of series after he took the hit during the Caston game.

"Cody was the captain of the defense and his job was to call our plays on the field," recalls Eli. "I remember Cody seeming a little fuzzy, after he took that hit. The guys in the huddle noticed something was a little off. There was a confused manner about Cody's speech, but that seemed to clear pretty quickly. After that, Cody appeared fine."

Another sign, in retrospect, was Cody's tardiness in making it to the team meeting the next morning. Eli remembers, "We were always the first two players to arrive for films the morning after a game. I was too young to drive, so Cody would pick me up on the way to practice. The morning after the Caston game, we were the last to arrive. Cody apologized to me, saying he just didn't feel good."

Cody knew he did not feel right. But he just did not comprehend the damage he could inflict by returning to play too quickly. A variety of thoughts likely clouded his judgment. He was a senior. This could be the final football game of his career. The doctor had encouraged him not to play, but the test the doctor had run showed that everything was OK.

It is easy to second guess Cody's decision to play, but he had no way of knowing how fragile his recovering brain was. If Cody had some indication that his choice would lead to his never graduating from high school, never walking again, and never being able to hold a job, I'm sure that Cody would have chosen differently. However, Cody was not granted such foresight, so he and his family must live with his decision each and every day.

In his initial concussive event, when Cody hit his Caston opponent, his cerebral cortex slammed forward hitting the ridges of his anterior skull, then rebounded back to the flat posterior skull resulting in a suction effect, as the brain moved back to midline. Axons were split, causing them to ball up and retract. The strong impact resulted in a significant number of neural disconnections. Cody's brain was still attempting to heal this damage when the minor hit in practice produced irrevocable injury.

After being airlifted to Methodist Hospital, in Indianapolis, Cody's brain was barely responding at a level to keep him alive. He was graded at a level 3 on the Glasgow Coma Scale. This is a common tool used to assess neurologically involved patients. It scores patients in the areas of eye opening response, verbal response, and motor response. Cody received one point in each realm, the lowest possible score. Cody was completely unresponsive to basic stimuli. The damage after the initial hit was repairable. However, upon the contact at practice, the damage was devastating.

Early in 2013, a case study was published in the <u>Journal of Neurosurgery: Pediatrics</u>; it details Cody's injury. Cody's case is particularly interesting to physicians and researchers, as he is the rare patient with a pre- and post-Second Impact Syndrome CT study with which to compare his injuries. According to information found in this journal article, Cody suffered from increased intracranial pressure, as noted in an MRI (Magnetic Resonance Imaging) taken upon Cody's arrival at Methodist Hospital. This pressure was caused by the brain's enlargement due to massive swelling. Herniation resulted, due to the subsequent lack of space within the skull. Imagery revealed subdural hematomas (bleeding below the outer protective layer) on both sides of the brain and downward herniation of the brain, including thalamus and hypothalamus.[16]

Referring to Figure 2 of the picture insert, there are three areas marked that could indicate a possible brain lesion (area affected by injury). If a lesion were to occur only at the cerebral cortex (A), the results are problematic, but usually only temporary. This area of insult would result in transient symptoms such as blurred vision, difficulty with speech, or difficulty concentrating. (These are often the outward signs of a concussion.)

If the lesion were to occur in the supracapsular region (B), only those specific fibers would be affected. For example, if an injury were to occur in the limbic system, deficits in learning would be noted, along with difficulty managing emotions and behaviors. No area of the brain functions in isolation. Thus, the deficits would not be as widespread, as the brain could compensate with input from other regions.

However, if the lesion were to occur at (C), the capsular region, all pathways that cross between the limbic region and basal ganglia would be affected. This would result in widespread complications. Many motor, speech, vision, memory, and even basic life functions would be compromised. In addition, these issues could present long-term challenges.[17] The brain's plasticity, or ability to create new pathways to heal itself, can only go so far. This is what happened in Cody's case, with the second hit at practice. If he had given himself time to recover from his initial concussion, Cody likely would have not have suffered any long-term effects.

There are no simple neural connections in the brain. It is not a basic system of input to one area of the brain resulting in directions being sent for output. There are layers upon layers of axons and neural pathways that send and receive messages in the brain. And, many areas of the brain are involved in each step. For example, there are multiple pathways that bring the sensory information to the cerebral cortex. Just as many pathways pass messages for motor response. Not only does the cerebral cortex receive this information for processing, the cerebellum is also aware of all internal and external information for the brain. Additionally, the limbic lobe also receives messages from these pathways to help the body prepare to respond to the movement. In this complex system, it is no wonder that a traumatic brain injury affects so many areas.

(Again, please refer back to Figure 2.) Think of the brain as a system of roadways. If a lesion occurs at (A), it is like a fender bender on a side-street in a neighborhood in the suburbs. An injury at (B) could be likened to an accident occurring on a stretch of highway from the suburb into the city. It can cause some traffic delays, but generally there is enough space to pass and avoid back-ups. On the other hand, a lesion occurring at (C) is similar to a car accident at a busy interchange on a downtown interstate, at rush hour. An accident here could cause significant congestion and snarl traffic for miles.

The human brain is an amazing network of cells. There are more than 100 billion neurons in the brain that work together to help us see, feel, run, read, think, and live. Like snowflakes, no two brains develop in exactly the same way. The human brain is like an ideal democracy. There are checks and balances, with many areas of the brain being aware of what is going on in other regions. There are areas of the brain that have specific duties, such as the basal ganglia for movement and the cerebellum for balance. Yet no region of the brain works in isolation. Rather, this system of neurons, synapses, and cells functions as a whole.

This presents challenges in regards to Cody's injury, as the herniation of portions of his brain affected not only those areas, but those that interacted with them. The good news is that many areas work to help different portions of the body function. Thus, when one area may be damaged, the brain will send out new synapses in order to bypass the damaged region. This neuroplasticity is what allows for improvements in traumatic brain-injured patients after injury. This, in combination with practice to learn to compensate for deficits, is what is built upon in physical therapy activities.

In summary, the brain is encased in the skull to provide it with protection from the typical misadventures of life. Concussions are a mild form of traumatic brain injury that occur when a blow, or blows, cause the brain to slosh around inside the skull. Concussions result in a cascade of chemical events that occur within the brain. This mild brain injury can result in various symptoms, from headaches to slowed thinking to vision challenges.

Typically, given time and opportunity to recover, the brain can repair itself. This requires a period of rest, without increased cognitive demands and away from television and computer screens. If a return to sports occurs before the brain is fully healed, it is more susceptible to further and often more serious injury.

CHAPTER 4

BEGINNING THERAPY

I first heard of Cody's injury through an article in the local newspaper. The Lafayette <u>Journal & Courier</u> had reported about Cody's accident and his subsequent road to recovery while he was in rehab in Indianapolis. After reading a story like Cody's, it is hard not to put yourself in the shoes of the family, and give your own children a bigger hug at night when you put them to bed. Later that spring, I was working with students at Tri-County High School for school-based therapy services, when I saw a flyer for a dance at the school. I read Cody's name and was reminded of his story. I was impressed that a school would be involved in a fundraiser for a student who was not their own. I thought that spoke highly of the students at Tri-County (another school in White County) and also of Cody, in that so many people would be interested in helping him.

Later that spring, I received a phone call from Pama Schreeg, the therapy director at Cooperative School Services. She said I would be receiving a referral for physical therapy services for Cody Lehe, once he had returned home from inpatient rehab. She indicated that this would likely be quite soon but that it might be for only a short period of time. Cody's family was working on another therapy option.

Due to his injury, Cody was unable to return to school that spring. Therefore, the school was responsible for providing homebound services for him. A teacher of record was established, but initially, Cody was not very responsive to any educational types of activities. Thus, speech, occupational, and physical therapies were Cody's initial educational services. As a related service in the educational setting, the role of physical therapy is to help the student access and participate in his or her school setting at the highest possible level.

Within the schools, I see students who have a classified disability. These classifications can be related to an orthopedic limitation such as muscular dystrophy or a cognitive challenge such as Down Syndrome, for example. At the schools, I work to help address positioning options for students in wheelchairs. I help school staff feel confident in transferring students who require assistance. I practice coordination skills with students to help enhance their participation in physical education activities, and I help practice safety on bus stairs, in busy hallways, and on the playground. In the homebound setting, my role is a little more broad. Since Cody's school setting was his home, all mobility, transfer training, balance activities, and family/teacher education were appropriate for me to address.

I was excited to work with Cody. Many of the children and young adults that I see for therapy have significant physical limitations, and thus, often make slow progress. On the other hand, patients recovering from a traumatic brain injury frequently make significant progress during the first 18 months of their recovery. The first time I pulled into the gravel drive of the Lehe farm, Cody was a little more than six months post-injury.

After parking, I walked to the newly constructed ramp leading to the front door of the white-sided house. Cody's mother answered the door. After introductions she led me into Cody's room, which had previously been the dining room. With the addition of a hospital bed and lots of pictures, it was now all Cody's. As I approached his bed, I glanced at the many photographs of the once healthy Cody. There were photos from baseball, basketball, and football. Cody's senior pictures stood in frames along one wall. A handsome young man with an engaging smile knelt in a field of wheat. In the picture, he was wearing a letter jacket with the Frontier "F" sewn onto the left side. That young man only bore a slight resemblance to the person who was lying in the bed looking back at me.

The Cody that I encountered that day had only just begun his rehab journey, even though he had recovered substantially from the life-threatening medical challenges. In April 2007, just a few weeks from his expected high school graduation ceremony, Cody required use of a Hoyer lift for transfers out of bed. He relied upon a reclining seat wheelchair for mobility. Cody demonstrated significant neglect of the left side of his body, and he required cues to perform any attempted reaching with his left hand. He also experienced challenges with his seated balance and had difficulty with speech and swallowing.

Cody was able to breathe without external assistance, but his tracheostomy collar remained. He did utilize it at night, to hook to a humidifier and a low level of oxygen. Cody was unable to vocalize, except with practice using a special device hooked to his tracheosotomy, called a Passy-Muir Valve.

The Cody that I first met in the spring of 2007 faced significant physical and mental challenges. Only years later did I learn how far Cody had already progressed to reach this, limited, point. Following his emergency airlift to Indianapolis, Cody had remained in a coma for several weeks. Once he was awake, things did not truly improve.

"We had issues with one major organ after another," Becky later explained.

Cody suffered from two collapsed lungs, a pneumothorax (trapped air in the chest that interferes with breathing), the loss of the tips of three toes (secondary to poor circulation), deep vein thrombosis (concern for blood clots), and kidney failure.

Cody underwent renal dialysis and had a filter placed in the blood vessels near his pelvis, among other procedures. Cody's family was unsure if he was going to survive. On Halloween (2006), Cody suffered a cardiac arrest that required two rounds of epinephrine along with two shocks with a defibrillator to resuscitate him.[18]

Family and friends were given updates of Cody's progress via mass emails on a nearly daily basis by family friend, Judi Brummett. Becky recently came across these emails, noting that she was both saddened by all that Cody had been through, but also encouraged, seeing how far he has come. These notes provide some insight into the challenges that faced Cody, early on.

(Tuesday, November 14, 2006, 10:30 a.m.)

"Hello, I have talked to Dale twice this morning and there is good news. Cody had another good night. The doctor was in, and when he pinched Cody, there was shoulder action and even eye movement, even though he hasn't opened them, yet. The doctors said that Cody is moving slowly, but no one should be alarmed because he is weak and his brain is still trying to recover. Daily improvement is GOOD! The arterial line is not in yet, but scheduled to be replaced. Cody's preliminary blood tests from the 11th and 12th for the blood infection came back negative, but they won't have true results until they have been allowed to grow for a couple of days. But it is looking good.

On the first call, Dale said that the doctors wanted to get another CAT Scan, but not until Cody was off the rotating bed. . . He called me back to tell me that they were going to be taking Cody off the rotating bed as soon as the air bed was delivered. They were also turning down the respirator and increasing his feeding amounts, because he needs increased nourishment. These are all GREAT signs, but Dale said they are also going to be trials to see if Cody can handle them.

Cody is a fighter; he's strong, and he will be waking up soon. Continue to keep him in your prayers because they are working. If I hear anything else, I will let you all know. Judi"

(Thursday November 30, 2006, 8:09 a.m.)

"We talked to Dale last night and Cody came through surgery (to remove fluid from his lungs) very well. He went in about an hour earlier than planned and it didn't take as long as expected. They got a lot more fluid extracted, than anticipated. He was back in his room around 4:30-5:00 and was resting comfortably. They did give him some sedatives to keep him comfortable to rest. Dale said that Cody had opened his eyes when he was in the room. He also said that his right lung was already expanded. He was on the respirator again due to the surgery, but Dale thought that would be short-term.

Earlier in the day, I talked to Becky and she mentioned that Cody has now lost 40 pounds. Dale assured her that it was all muscle loss and he could get it back. Needless to say, their spirits were better after Cody was out of surgery. I will be calling them later this morning to find out how Cody did through the night. Keep praying for him and hopefully this will be the turning point for him to speedily improve!!!! Judi"

Cody remained in the critical care unit (CCU) of Methodist Hospital until the first part of January, 2007. His family saw the symbolism in the number of days he had remained in the CCU: 55, the number he wore on his football jersey. Cody transitioned to the rehab unit at Methodist, as he was not medically stable enough to return home. Yet, Cody had not recovered, physically or mentally to a level where he could truly participate in a rehab setting.

After 30 days, Dale and Becky sat in a room with 18 medical professionals who suggested that Cody be transferred to an extended care facility (nursing home), so that he could regain his strength and continue his rehabilitation, there. The hospital staff indicated that this would be the best placement for Cody and would allow Becky and Dale to return to a more typical life at home with their two younger children,

Abbey and Zach. Becky told them that they would do no such thing. They were a family, and they would be taking Cody home, if that is what needed to happen.

So in early February 2007, on the weekend that Cody turned 18 and the Indianapolis Colts won the Super Bowl, the whole Lehe family headed home. There was some celebrating over each event, but not for long. The transition to home was a challenging one. A ramp was quickly constructed. A hospital bed, with an inflatable mattress that rotated to assist respiration and circulation, was delivered, and family members were trained to help care for Cody.

Another email from Judi Brummett describes how things were unfolding for the Lehes back at home:

> *(Friday, February 2, 2007, 11:58 a.m.)*
> *"... Just off the phone with Becky and she said that things are going pretty well. They have had two good nights, and Cody seems to like being at home. Before they left the hospital, the nurse put a valve in Cody's trach opening that could take air in, but would allow him to blow it out so that he could make sounds. She said that after saying 'Mom' the day before, she told Cody that he couldn't leave his dad out, so she asked him to say 'Dad', and he did.*
>
> *They are still getting schedules for therapy and nursing staff set up. They are hoping that a routine develops by next week. Becky sounded great!!!!! She did say that when they are all in the kitchen eating dinner and talking, Cody gets to huffing and puffing because he is being left out. So, they relocate around him and retell the stories. She said that the TV in the dining room, where Cody is at, is getting better reception than the one in the living room, so they all sit in there with Cody to watch TV. She said he does really well holding his head up now, too.*

Becky said that Cody is really coherent about what they are asking him and he is trying to communicate with mouth movement. She said that when he looks at her and Dale, it is really him. What great news. She wanted you all to know that he is improving. Abbey (Cody's sister) got her driver's license yesterday. Hurray, also!!! Becky said it felt good to be home together.

Again, Cody's birthday is on Saturday, so send him a birthday wish/prayer. Take care and I will keep you posted.

Cody is our MIRACLE in progress!!!! Judi"

In addition to the many thoughts and prayers, the community of White County community came together to help support the Lehes. Several respiratory therapists volunteered their services to check in with Cody, and a neighbor who is a nurse provided family support, as well. Frontier High School produced magnets that read: "Cody Lehe: #55 Tough Enough." Meals were prepared to help keep the Lehe family functioning at home. Various fundraisers were organized to help cover Cody's mounting medical expenses. These included, but were not limited to a "salon-a-thon" (hair-cutting fundraiser at Cody's aunt's business), a golf outing, a raffle, a bingo night, the Tri-County dance which was attended by students from at least seven local schools, and a chicken noodle dinner. The White County REMC donated money to Cody's fund through Operation Round-Up, and several thousand dollars were raised when a Frontier football helmet was passed at a gathering at The Top-Notch restaurant in Brookston.

When I arrived for my first visit, I was aware of Cody's medical history, but I had no idea of what he and his family had already been through. I was only able to see Cody for two visits before he had progressed sufficiently to be accepted back to Methodist Hospital for inpatient rehabilitation. This time, Cody could participate in his rehab setting at a higher level. I was glad that he was able to receive this more intense service. It was appropriate for him at the time, and his level of function hopefully would improve with this increased level of therapies.

Judi Brummett's ongoing email updates indicate Cody's level of progress, as he returned to the rehab unit:

(Thursday, April 26, 2007, 11:17 a.m.)
"Becky and Dale took Cody to Methodist on Monday for an evaluation on his progress. It went very well. They weren't as interested in his cognitive abilities, as they were his physical. Becky thought the clincher was when Cody sat on the edge of the bed to help get his shirt off, then back on. He really wants to get out of bed, go outside, and sleep in his own room. So, they think he is very determined to get better. He continues to improve daily. He is talking in full sentences, itching the back of his head, making the sign of the cross, but also pulling on his trach. Hopefully that will come out soon. Cody still can't comprehend that he was in the hospital for three months and has been home for two. He asked Becky whose legs were on the bed. She told him they were his, and he disagreed. But, when she asked him to move his foot, he did. The doctors and therapist said that is very typical as the body continues to wake up. ..
... Becky is so excited and I am sure that Dale and the rest of the family are also. Becky will be staying down at rehab with Cody, and helping with the therapy. That means that Dale and the kids will probably be home tending to the daily grind of planting season and school/ sports. It might be necessary for us to pitch in again and make sure there is food for them. Dale will be very busy as soon as the fields dry up . . ."

After one month in inpatient rehab, Cody returned home, in part so that Becky could be closer to the rest of the family. Over the next seven months, Becky would drive Cody to Lafayette Home Hospital for rehabilitation services five days a week. There, Cody would participate in three hours of therapies each day. He would practice oral motor activities to help improve his swallowing. Tongue-movement strategies for speech activities began, since Cody no longer had his tracheostomy. Activities such as rolling and reaching would be practiced in occupational therapy. Also, Cody would practice daily living skills such as brushing his teeth and transferring to a toilet. In physical therapy, Cody would practice transitioning from lying down to sitting. Once sitting, he worked on maintaining his balance. He began transitioning to stance and developing stability in this upright posture. Basically, Cody had to relearn all of the basic life skills he had developed as an infant and young child.

By December 2007, just over one year after his head injury, Cody was transferring to standing with moderate assistance, and beginning to walk with the aid of two people. His speech gains were significant, also, and his sense of humor had returned. At this point, Becky began to notice what a funny young man Cody was.

"I initially thought that Cody's sense of humor was heightened after his accident," says Becky. "But, as people began telling me more and more stories of the 'old Cody,' I realized that he just hadn't shared this side of himself, with his mother, in high school."

Cody's motor skill level continued to progress, and his family was interested in pursuing another inpatient rehab setting. They felt he had reached a stable level of health and could benefit from more intense, inpatient services. After much work and prior approval, Becky and Cody planned their move to Carbondale, Illinois. At this inpatient rehab setting, Cody was able to receive ongoing therapy services with an emphasis on functional self-care, in an apartment setting. Cody was able to interact with other young men and women who had been through a similar experience (TBI), and likely for the first time since the accident, Cody had not felt "different" from his peers.

However, therapy services were not consistent, due to maternity leaves, and Becky could not rationalize being away from her family any longer, when Cody had been receiving such good outpatient services close to home. Abbey and Zach were now both in high school an involved in a variety of sports and activities. Dale was placed in charge of all of the Lehe home activities. Everyone managed, but it was quite challenging for each family member. Dale felt like he was constantly on the run with the other two Lehe children, while Becky felt she was missing out on a lot at home.

In addition to sister Abbey and brother Zach, Cody also has two older half-sisters, Kylee in California and Kinsey nearby in Delphi, Indiana. At the time of Cody's accident, Abbey was a sophomore at Frontier, and Zach was in the eighth grade. Not only was Cody's world upended with the hit on the football field, the whole family was impacted.

When I returned to Cody's home in the spring of 2008, he was a very different young man. He had a strong vocabulary, and his motor skills had advanced as well. Cody had progressed to the point that his family was considering trading in his handicap-accessible van for a more (as Cody put it) "pimped-out ride". Cody was transferring well enough that his mother was considering a vehicle where Cody could sit in the front seat, and fold the wheelchair into the back.

"It's much easier to cruise for girls that way," Cody later told me.

When I entered Cody's room this time, he was sitting up in his wheelchair. His face no longer drooped on the left side, and he was much more animated.

"What's up," he asked as I walked toward his chair.

"Hey, Cody," I greeted him, "it's been a while ... My name is Jim. I'm a physical therapist. I don't know if you remember me."

"I think I might be remembering you," Cody replied. He reached out to shake my hand.

I met his hand. This turned into an intricate series of grasps, slides, and snaps, ultimately culminating in a quick spreading of the fingers, while making an explosive sound. It took me a few tries, but I had seen similar handshakes before, though none quite like Cody's. After the third attempt, Cody concurred that I had acceptably completed the handshake.

"Let me hear your explosion again," he requested.

"Bbqueww." I gave it my best sound effect.

"That was pretty good," Cody replied. "Now, move your arms apart when you make the sound."

I complied, evidently to Cody's satisfaction.

"Mom, you have got to see this," Cody shouted, as his mother returned to the room.

"Cody," I replied, "I will give you another handshake, but first let's practice some standing. We need something to explode about." And so our physical therapy sessions began, again.

CHAPTER 5

MEMORY

There is a light breeze blowing over the infield grass of Gordon Lemming Field, on this spring day in 2006. But that breeze does little to cool the humid air or to ease the tension in the opening game of the Indiana Class A Baseball Sectionals, between the Frontier Falcons and the Central Catholic Knights. These teams have met in the sectional games for the past three years, with Central Catholic advancing on to the regional round each time. Now in his junior year, Cody and his teammates have decided that this result will be different.

It has been a terrific game, with Frontier having the better of it. The score is 12-11, as the Frontier catcher walks calmly to the pitcher's mound. It is the bottom of the ninth inning. The bases are loaded and the count is full. This is what the Falcons have worked toward all season.

The pitcher is understandably a little on edge, so Cody tries to diffuse the situation for him. "Hey, Sam," says Cody, "you know what that batter just told me?" The Falcon pitcher shakes his head at his friend, to indicate he has no idea. "Well, he said that when you were born, you were so ugly, that the doctor slapped your momma. Now let's not let him get away with that. Strike this guy out and let's go home!"

These were the situations that Cody lived for. He gives a knowing look at the batter, as he settles in behind the plate. Cody signals for a fast ball. The fans for both sides are on their feet. Players cheer from the edge of their dugouts. Cody positions his glove on the inside corner

35

of the plate, and waits for Sam to deliver ... Strike three! Cody rushes the mound to join his team in celebration.

The Falcon baseball team went on to capture the sectional and regional crowns, only to lose in the championship game of the semi-state. What a great memory this would be, if only Cody could recall the event. Memories are important parts of who we are and provide the framework of our personalities. Unfortunately, Cody's brain injury has impacted both his short-term and long-term memories, forever.

55   55   55   55   55   55   55   55   55   55   55   55   55   55

"Don't tell my hamstrings, my achey, breaky hamstrings. I just don't think they'd understand," I sing the remainder of the chorus in a horrible, off-key manner, with Cody providing the "wooo- hoo" at the end. With apologies to Billy Ray Cyrus, I bully the song enough to distract Cody from the hamstring stretches we are performing on the floor, in preparation for his physical therapy session.

And it works. Cody was three years old when Miley Cyrus' father made that song famous. Yet, Cody is able to sing along with me for the majority of it, even filling in words that I have forgotten. This is the mystery of Cody's memory. Likely, Cody has not heard this song more than a time or two in his life, but he is able to recall the majority of it.

Yet there are times when he struggles to recall the name of his younger brother. Cody's memory does remain limited, especially the part that translates bits of information for storage. Recently, Becky injured her finger while helping Cody transfer at an exercise facility. It had bruised by the time I had arrived that afternoon, and when I noticed it, I asked what had happened.

Once she explained, a sad look crossed Cody's face. "I'll sure be bein' awfully sorry, Mom," he says.

Becky smiles, with sympathy in her eyes. "Cody, it will be okay. You know that it was just an accident, and you must have apologized about 100 times already today."

"I have?" asks Cody, "Well, then I guess I won't go on feeling quite as bad." And this was true, until about 45 minutes later, when Cody noticed his mother's finger again, and asks her what had happened.

The memory process is not completely understood. One theory is that reverberations occur in the circuitry of a specific part of the brain, called the cerebral cortex. When these reverberations slow or new signals interfere with them, memories fade. A blow to the head can disrupt this circuitry and cause a loss of short-term memory.[19] Long-term memory is more durable and can be maintained despite ischemia (lack of blood flow), hypoxia (lack of oxygen) or other events. Short-term memory allows you to remember where you left the car keys. Long-term memory helps you recall who the first president was.

When a new memory develops, it is first encoded or registered. Then, it is stored, and lastly it must be retrieved. New short-term memories may be difficult to register and store if areas of the brain are damaged. Long-term memories, having already been established, are generally more accessible to someone who has suffered a TBI. Yet, they may still be challenging to retrieve.

For over three years, from 2008-2011, I typically saw Cody twice a week for physical therapy services. Each time I arrived, Cody and I would go through the same dance. Cody would hear someone at the door, and his mother would ask him who he thinks it could be, as I enter the foyer.

"What's it start with?" he asks.

"Oh, Cody, you know who it is," replies Becky. And he does. But there are days that I see a flicker of recognition, but still uncertainty.

Some days, I will wait until Cody answers. Other days, I will make up a new name. I have been "Rufus Xavier Zanfrarilla, Wilfred Sigmund McGhee, and Savoufaire McGuillicuty". Remarkably, Cody can guess these names as quickly as he can recall "Jim Cooley."

"What name were you born with?" asks Cody, nearly every visit.

"James," I reply.

"Have you ever been called Jimmy?" he asks.

"By my aunts, when I was little," I reply, "and it happened again, this past Monday."

"Who called you Jimmy?" Cody asks.

"Oh, it was some guy, with the initials C.L. that lives near Brookston," I respond.

"Huh?" says Cody. Then after a beat, he laughs. "Was that me?" he chuckles, then says, "Jim, how do you do it? You are a funny man."

And so it goes visit after visit. Cody struggling to remember, but there are glimmers of recall intermixed. Recently I have been called "Jimmy Fuego." I have no idea where the "Fuego" comes from. I'm not sure Cody does, either. But I like it and it appears to have stuck. Cody's speech therapist consistently works with him on memory activities. One day, at a visit, she asked him questions about me, his school physical therapist.

I have never met Cody's speech therapist, and she does not know any significant information about me. So, she had to rely upon Cody for the validity of the information he was providing. By the time Cody was done, he had convinced her that I was originally from Nova Scotia. I think that I could find Nova Scotia on a globe, if given enough time. But, I have certainly never been there, let alone spent my childhood there. Perhaps, I could visit some day. Cody assures me that it is a nice place.

For a short-term memory to be translated to a long-term memory, nerve synapses must be facilitated for a range of 5 minutes up to an hour.[20] A concussion or injury to the brain makes this consolidation challenging. Damage to the intricate system that composes one's memories makes it difficult to recall recent thoughts or experiences, to compose new ideas, or to act upon old ideas.

Studies have shown the hippocampus plays an important role in memory. There are two hippocampi, which are located beneath the cerebral cortex. One role of the hippocampus appears to be in aiding the brain to translate short-term memories into long-term ones. Neural connections within the hippocampi decline as a person ages, which explains why memory issues frequently present a challenge for the elderly. The hippocampi are known to become damaged in such cognitive impairments as Alzheimer's Disease.

Dr. Thomas Talavage, a professor of electrical and computer engineering at Purdue University, and an expert in neuroimaging, was able to take an MRI of Cody's brain approximately three years ago. He found an increase in cerebrospinal fluid (CSF) surrounding Cody's cerebral cortex meninges, which provides detail to the extent of Cody's injury. The greater amount of CSF in this area of the brain indicates the amount of shrinkage caused by the damage in various regions of the brain. Specifically, Dr. Talavage noted that Cody's hippocampi were extremely damaged and were almost absent in diagnostic studies.[21] This explains Cody's challenges in short-term memory. The hippocampus plays an important role in forming and storing memories. People with extensive damage of both hippocampi often suffer from anterograde amnesia. This refers to the inability to form and retain new memories.

One physical therapy visit to the Lehe household exemplifies this memory issue. I arrived at Cody's house on the Monday following his birthday. "Hey, Cody," I greet him, "how was your weekend? Did you do anything exciting?"

After watching Cody ponder for a moment, with no look of recognition, Becky offers some hints. "We had a cake and pizza. . . Some of your friends stopped by to celebrate. . ."

"Was it my birthday?" Cody asks excitedly. "How old am I? Eighteen?"

Becky responds, "Higher."

"Nineteen?"

"Higher."

"Twenty?"

"Higher."

Cody is becoming even more excited, as he knows he must be getting close. "Twenty-one?" he shouts.

"Higher," answers his mother.

"Twenty-two?"

Becky nods, and Cody becomes more exuberant. "Does that mean that I can … (he raises his hand as if holding a cup to take a drink) … ya' know? DRINK BEER?"

Becky laughs and replies, "It does. You even had a beer on your birthday."

"What kind was it?" asks Cody.

After pausing for a moment to consider, his mother answers, "Blue Moon."

Both Becky and I roll our eyes as Cody breaks into song. "Blue moon … you saw me standing alone … without a love in my heart … without a love of my own …"

Songs play a remarkable role in Cody's rehabilitation. The music helps to keep him entertained, but the lyrics can also be altered to help him retain information. Cody's half-sister had a baby boy over the summer, and Cody was having the hardest time remembering his name. So, he had to come up with a song to help him with this recall. Ask Cody the name of his new nephew, and he would sing you a verse of this song, sung to the tune of "Mary Had a Little Lamb".

"Kylee had a little baby, little baby, little baby. Kylee had a little baby, and his name was Simon Liam."

But, after a few weeks, he was able to consolidate this short-term memory into a long-term one, so that the song was no longer necessary. Cody's brain injury makes memory a challenge, but with practice he is able to work with other, non-damaged areas, in order to compensate.

55   55   55   55   55   55   55   55   55   55   55   55   55   55

"Who is that?" Cody asks as his sister enters the kitchen, where we are practicing some sidestepping.

"I'm not sure," I reply. "But, I think you might be able to remember her name."

"Give me a clue," Cody says.

"She has the same last name as your brother," I answer.

"Is it Abatha?" whispers Cody.

I nod, then he shouts. "Hey Abatha! Good to see you."

Cody's memory is a remarkable adventure. There are gaping holes, which must thoroughly frustrate him; and then there are those clear windows. We are playing a game of "Guess Who," to help keep Cody motivated while we are continuing with the sidestepping activities. Abatha, or Abbey, as she is called by everyone else, is still in the kitchen.

"Is your person a girl?" asks Cody. I answer and he knocks down the appropriate pieces, while working on his standing balance.

"Does your person have eyebrows?" I ask (some of the characters' eyebrows are covered by hair or a hat).

Cody laughs, but Abbey says, "There was a boy that rode our bus who was born without eyebrows. I can't remember his name."

"Cody can you remember who it was?" his mother asks.

Without missing a beat, Cody answers, "Yep. That was David Hall."

Becky, Abbey, and I nearly fall to the floor. After the shock wears off, we all share a good laugh, even Cody.

"How in the world can you remember that?" I ask Cody.

He shrugs his shoulders and replies, "Who'll be knowin'?"

And who will be knowing? How can the same young man, who just three minutes earlier could not recall his own sister's name without a series of clues, remember the name of a boy who rode his school bus in the fifth grade? Who will be knowin', indeed?

Dealing with and understanding memory deficits – and how to minimize them – are some of the most challenging portions of Cody's ongoing recovery efforts. Memory is a very complex network. The network, which can be damaged at many variable points, is responsible for memory storage and retrieval. And that recall, in Cody's case, can be circumnavigated by song. Just as Cody is able to remember his nephew's name through the use of music, Cody is able to recall more songs than many people have ever heard. His palate is variable, from rap to country, from popular to classic rock.

"Whatever is on the radio," Becky says. "Cody can hear a song once, and he'll be singing it all day." And Cody does not just sing the chorus, he sings the full song.

As Cody's short-term memory presents a challenge in areas such as academics and safety, it also affects his gross motor progress. Relatively simple activities -- such as organizing how to swing away his wheelchair leg rests -- have proven a challenge for Cody to motor plan. It took nearly 1 ½ years of practice to master this activity.

Today, Cody is quickly able to set up his wheelchair in preparation for a transfer.

"Brakes on!" he shouts in the accent of Mr. Miyagi from the movie Karate Kid. Then, he skillfully pushes the release button on each side of the swing-away leg rests. He completes the whole process in less than 10 seconds.

However, there was a time not so long ago, when this process seemed monumental. Each time Cody attempted to find the wheelchair leg rest release, it seemed like the first time he had encountered the task. The next time that he was asked to attempt the same activity, Cody had no recall of any prior experience from which to draw. For Cody, it was like asking a carpenter to build an elaborate house, but then taking away the blueprint.

In an effort to help Cody learn the skill of moving his wheelchair leg rests out of the way for transfers, we marked the releases with colored tape, in hopes that this would make the release easier to locate. While Cody knew he was looking for something to press, in order to maneuver the foot supports, he wasn't quite sure where to begin his search.

Over time and with constant repetition, Cody was eventually able to learn this important functional skill. In this case, short-term memory was able to translate into long-term recall through perseverance. Perhaps, if I had thought to develop a song to assist Cody in developing management skills for his wheelchair, this could have happened more quickly and with far fewer curse words.

Cody uses a song to the tune of "You Are My Sunshine" to help him remember the days he goes to Lafayette for his workouts. "At 10 a.m. on Tuesday/Thursday, I go see Martha at Rosewalk Village. I do a workout on the treadmill. Sometimes bike and upper body too. Boom! Boom!" Cody ends the song with a chuckle that is contagious.

"Don't you just love it?" he asks.

I nod in agreement. Of course I love it. How could I not? I keep thinking that I need to come up with a theme song for physical therapy. I am still looking for just the right tune.

While Cody's bits and pieces of memory are a mystery, sometimes his lack of short-term memory is a boon to working through challenging activities in therapy.

"Mom, why is he here?" shouts Cody, red-faced as he points at me.

His mother patiently responds, "Jim is here to help you with your walking. You know how you want to put away your wheelchair. Well, you have to practice your walking, just like you practiced football, to get better."

"Well, when is he going to leave?" Cody asks somewhat more calmly.

"He'll only be here for a little while longer," replies Becky. "So, get to work and I'll make you some hot tea for when you finish."

On this day, I have been working with Cody for nearly 45 minutes, and his agitation is a result of me pushing him just a little too far. I generally have a pretty good gauge of how hard we can work. But occasionally, when the activity is going well, or I see an area that requires some practice, I push just a little further. On these occasions, when Cody is challenged, is when he makes the most improvement. Unfortunately, it is also when we see more agitation.

This is one time when Cody's memory issues come in handy. No matter how mad Cody gets, given a little distraction, he will forget that he was mad in the first place, and we can get back to work.

"When are you leaving?" Cody grimaces.

"As soon as we're done with therapy," I respond.

"When will that be?" he asks, still perturbed.

"Fifteen more minutes, Cody, we're almost finished. Do you know how to say that in Spanish?" I ask. After waiting a few seconds with no response from Cody, I answer, "Quince minutas." Although I am fairly sure that this is incorrect, I am hoping to distract Cody enough to return to his therapy activities.

"Quince minutas," chuckles Cody, "Where did you learn that?"

"Senora Hernandez," I answer. "She was my Spanish teacher in high school. She also taught me: 'Voy a la officina. Que' tal. Muy bien. Gracias.'"

"What in the world does that mean?" Cody asks, in slightly better spirits.

"It means: I am going to the office," I respond. "How is it going? I am well. Thank you."

"I still don't know what in the world you are talking about," Cody laughs. "But that is a good one, Jim. How in the world do you do it?"

And so the earlier frustration is forgotten and we get back to work for the final 14 minutes of Cody's physical therapy session.

When Cody returned from his inpatient rehab stay in Illinois, his walking pattern had improved to the point that he could at least practice it intermittently. His ambulation required a significant amount of assistance, and it was not yet a skill that we emphasized on a daily basis in physical therapy sessions. There were other more basic skills that needed to be developed. We did practice walking, on occasion, to help keep Cody motivated and encourage his continued progress toward this functional skill.

Approximately six months later, in early 2009, Cody had received his new left AFO (ankle foot orthosis). This brace which extends from the bottom of his foot to his calf, provides support and stability to Cody's ankle. A hinge at the ankle allows some flexibility. When Cody is walking with assistance, the AFO facilitates Cody to clear his toes in advancement of the lower leg. Cody began making more gains in his walking skills, but, similar to the challenge encountered in learning how to use his leg rest release, Cody experienced difficulty in learning to advance his walker.

The advancement of a walker is similar to the steps of a waltz: ... "1,2,3 ... 1,2,3". On 1, the user advances the walker forward. On 2, the weaker or more tonally involved leg advances inside the walker. Then on 3, the other leg advances even with the first. It is a simple pattern – one that is easily learned by every patient who undergoes a total knee or hip replacement. However, with Cody, anything that requires short-term memory does not come easily. And with these challenges comes frustration. It was difficult for Cody to remember when to advance the walker, or to recall which foot (the left) to swing forward first. When he took the correct foot forward, he could not remember to avoid advancing it too far.

During this time, Cody was typically watching a Chuck Norris television show when I arrived for my Thursday afternoon physical therapy session. In the show, Norris played a Texas Ranger named Walker. So, one day, as Cody was becoming frustrated over the sequencing pattern for ambulation, I decided to utilize the name of this TV program to help stir Cody's memory.

"Cody, do you remember the name of the TV show you were watching when I got here?" I ask.

"What show was that?" he responds earnestly.

"The Texas Ranger program," I reply.

"Oh yeah, I do like that," he responds.

"Yeah," I counter, "that Walker is one tough hombre. How about we use that show to help us with your walking?"

"That would be totally pimped up," Cody answers.

I take that as an affirmative, and explain how we might accomplish this task. I stand inside the walker to demonstrate my plan.

"Walker," as I advance the walker appropriately in front of myself. "Texas is the left foot," as I step forward with my left leg. "And, Ranger is the right foot," as I advance even with my other leg. I proceed for a few more steps. "Walker ... Texas ... Ranger," I step evenly with my chorus, "Walker ... Texas ... Ranger."

I bring the walker to Cody and help him to stand. Although it takes him a few tries to recall which leg is Texas and which is Ranger, he immediately begins to remember to advance his walker before taking a step forward. I'm sure Becky is trying to stifle a laugh as Cody makes his way into the kitchen, while shouting "Walker ... Texas ... Ranger" with gusto.

But, it works. Just as singing aids in Cody's recall, this silly mantra makes something "click" in his short-term memory. Cody began using the chant whenever he would walk. After a few months, he no longer required the verbal cues to complete the pattern. I have to admit that I sometimes miss calling out the name of that '90s television program as Cody practices walking.

For Christmas that year, one of Cody's outpatient therapists presented Cody with a t-shirt she had discovered online. At my next visit after the holidays Cody proudly wore his gift. On the front was a drawing of a walker, wearing a cowboy hat and a badge. Under the picture, in large, bold letters, it read: "Walker, Texas Ranger." Kudos to his outpatient therapist for finding it!

CHAPTER 6

THE FREEZE

On a recent birthday, Cody received a special hat. It is similar to the beer-drinking helmets that one might find at variety stores, with a container on each side. A straw dangles from each cup. This particular hat was modified to fit Cody. In addition to the "Code-Fly" nickname affixed to the front, there was also lettering inscribed above each beverage container. One side was labeled "The Melt" and the other "The Freeze."

The person who created this hat for Cody obviously knows him quite well. Since his brain injury, Cody has been challenged with thermoregulation. There is rarely a time, when Cody feels comfortable, in regard to temperature: He is either hot or cold. And this is not the garden-variety, "Gosh it is a little bit chilly in here."

Cody describes the "freeze" as feeling, "Colder than a witch's . . . Jim you know the rest."

"Yes, Cody I do," I reply, "but, I like my job and I think I might lose it, if I complete your sentence."

"Jim, how do you do it?" Cody laughs.

The hypothalamus serves as the thermostat for the body. Within this portion of the brain are heat and cold-sensitive neurons that fire when exposed to heat and cold. These neurons receive information from various parts of the body, from the skin to core-temperature sensors. The body then responds with vasodilation (expansion of blood vessels) and/or sweating to help cool the body. Or, if needed it responds with vasoconstriction (narrowing of blood vessels) and/or heat production.

Since Cody's injury, his hypothalamus has not been a consistent regulator. He is generally cold and cannot get warm no matter what he does. At these times it is difficult for Cody to think of anything other than how cold he is feeling. On some occasions, when he is lucky, the cold "breaks" and Cody feels hot. There are not any occasions where Cody is comfortable at a "normal" resting temperature. The warmth, however, is more tolerable, as he can remove a sweatshirt or ingest a cold drink to beat the heat.

Like most people who travel south for spring break, Cody prefers the warm temperatures to the cold. Becky can always gauge how Cody's day is going to unfold by the temperature of the drink he requests. Cody prefers to drink water, and he either asks for it hot or cold. Unfortunately for Cody and his family, he asks for hot water more frequently than cold. When Cody is in the "freeze" he tends to be more uncomfortable -- and hence, more grumpy.

The "melt" and the "freeze" are terms, aptly named by Cody to describe how he feels at a given time. These terms come from the holiday classic, "The Year Without a Santa Claus," and of course for Cody, relate to a song.

During a recent visit, Cody sings, "I'm Mr. Freeze Miser. I'm Mr. Cold. I'm Mr. ..."

Cody holds his hand out to pass the song on to me. I sing the remainder of the verse, "White Christmas. I'm Mr. 20 Below."

Back to Cody, "Friends call me Freeze Miser. Whatever I touch, turns to ice in my clutch."

Again my turn, "Doo, doot, doo, I'm too much. Doo, doot, doo."

And Cody brings it home with a big finish, "Too much!"

But, generally Cody's lack of warmth does not put him in the mood to sing. "Mom, pllleeze get me out of this 'freeze,'" Cody says as he sits with his sweatshirt on.

"Just work hard with Jim," replies his mother. Looking at her son, she adds, "When you get a good workout, it warms you up. Hopefully, that will help you out of the 'freeze.'"

And, sometimes it does. Invariably, Cody works up a good sweat. And, on good days, he enters the "melt" and I leave him in a better mood than when I arrived. One such case occurred recently.

"How are you doing today?" I ask Cody, while removing my jacket, and placing it on the chair beside the kitchen table.

Cody shrugs, with a grimace on his face. "OK," he replies, "just freezing bootoff, though."

"Bootoff?" I ask, realizing I need to change the tone of this visit, if we are going to get some work done. "That sounds like the last name of the Russian gentleman who just bought the New Jersey Nets."

"Bootoff," chuckles Cody.

"Yes," I reply. "What would be a good Russian first name for Mr. Bootoff? How about Ivan?"

"Ivan Bootoff?" asks Cody. "Nah, I would prefer a name that rhymes."

"You know a name that rhymes with Bootoff?" I ask, surprised.

"Sure," responds Cody, "Gustav."

"Gustav Bootoff," I repeat. "I like it. Middle name: Freezing."

"Gustav Freezing Bootoff," laughs Cody.

"Yes," I respond, "That will be your name today. Now let's get to work, Mr. Bootoff."

And, so we do.

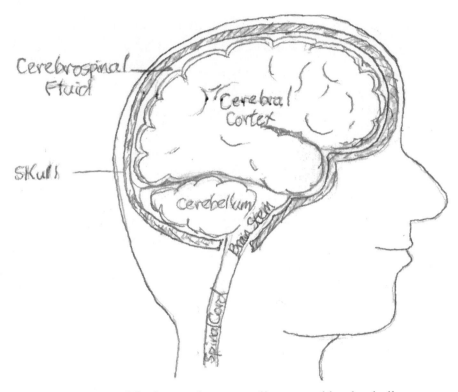

Figure 1: The human brain is well-protected by the skull, dura, and cerebrospinal fluid. However, large impacts can result in movement and injury of this vital organ.

Coronal Section of the Brain

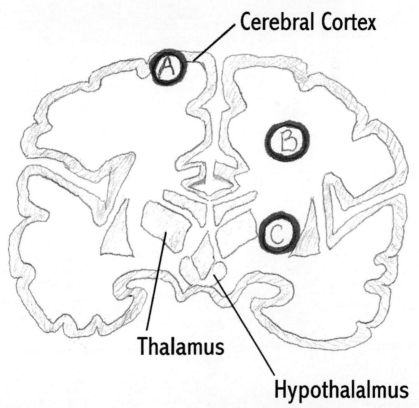

Figure 2: In this cross section of the brain, injuries that occur at (A) are problematic but generally resolve quickly. At (B) injuries might be more pronounced but primarily impact only that area of the brain. While at (C), many pathways are affected resulting in significant and variable injury.

Cody's family: (front row left to right) Simon, Andrew, Cody, Kylee,
(back row) Dale, Zach, Abbey, Becky, Kinsey, and Aaron.

Cody lining up to play center during a game in his senior season.
He also played linebacker and was a captain of the defense.

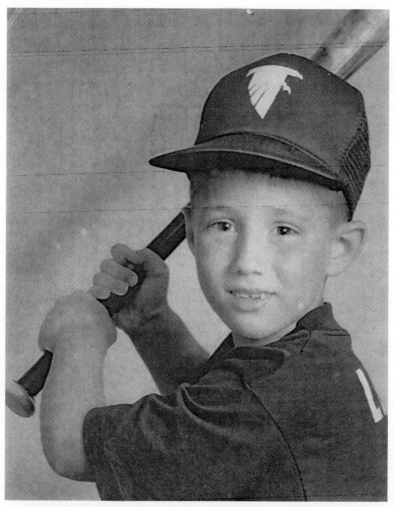

While Cody loved to play football, he may have been even more talented in the sport of baseball. Here is Cody at age 9, as a member of the Frontier little league baseball team.

Cody and Lindsay before prom during their junior year.

Cody Patrick Lehe

Parents: Dale and Becky Lehe
Sisters: Kylee, Kinsey, Abbey
Brother: Zach
Birthday: February 4, 1989

Sports:

> **Freshman:** Varsity Football, JV Basketball, JV Baseball
> **Sophomore:** Varsity Football, JV Basketball, Varsity Baseball
> **Junior:** Varsity Football, Varsity Basketball, Varsity Baseball
> **Senior:** Varsity Football, Varsity Basketball, Varsity Baseball

Clubs: FFA, 4 H
Community Activities: St Joseph Church Youth Group
Awards/Achievements: Football-2004 and 2006 All White County, 2006 All Conference, 2006 Victor Dykhuizen Award
Hobbies: Athletics, farming, video games
Future Plans: Study Agriculture in college and also play football

Cody's senior picture along with a list of his many
high school achievements and activities.

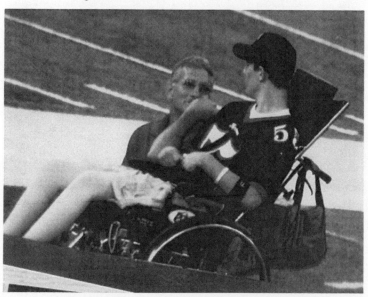

Cody and Dale watching Zach play football
in the RCA Dome, fall of 2007.

Cody and Jim during a physical therapy session working
on weight-shifting at the "swim-up bar."

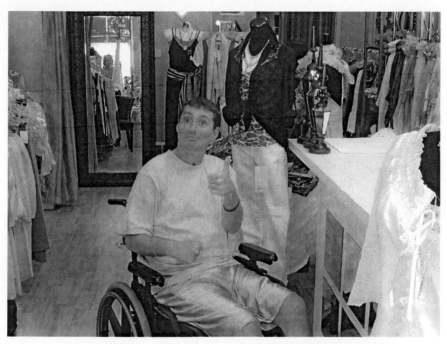

Cody hard at work at his mother's shop, *B Boutique* or
as Cody calls it: "Rebecca Sue's Bou-Ti-Q."

CHAPTER 7

HELP! SOMEONE HAS BROKEN INTO MY HOUSE AND IS FORCING ME TO EXERCISE

When I worked at the hospital, some of our patients insisted that PT (physical therapy) stood for pain and torture. While Cody does not experience much pain, aside from some tightness during hamstring and hip flexor stretches, I'm sure he would agree with the torture aspect of physical therapy.

In the year 2010, I visit Cody two times each week for 60-minute physical therapy sessions. He also currently attends one outpatient physical therapy session at Fransciscan St. Elizabeth Health, in Lafayette. Additionally, he performs directed exercise at Rosewalk Village, also in Lafayette. There he takes advantage of their equipment, including weight machines and a treadmill, under direct supervision.

There is a story that I enjoy that may in fact be an urban legend. But, I will share it just the same, because it is likely how Cody feels when I travel to his home on Monday mornings and Thursday afternoons. The story goes that a homecare physical therapist had traveled to see an elderly patient for an initial visit, as prescribed by her physician. For the purpose of this story, we will say that she was recovering from some weakness related to a bout of pneumonia. The patient answered the door, but she could not understand why the therapist was there. She begrudgingly let the therapist in, but after a brief explanation of the plans for the visit, she asked the therapist to step out of the room. Then, unbeknownst to the PT, the elderly patient called 911 and frantically explained that someone had broken into her home and was trying to force her to exercise.

True story or not, I understand the woman's perspective. She had not signed up for this program; neither has Cody. So, on given days I am met with less than a warm reception. This is infrequent but definitely understandable. I am intruding into Cody's home, and as far as he is concerned, I am uninvited. Plus, I have come to force him to exercise.

"Mom, why do I have to do this stuff?" Cody might say when I push him too hard. Or, "Mom, when is this guy leaving?" Or, "This stanks!"

I usually have a simple answer for each of these questions. And, in this case, Cody's limited short-term memory can work to my advantage. I can give the same answer to these frequently asked questions, and it is as if Cody is hearing it for the first time. So, when I find an answer that strikes Cody as humorous and that distracts him from his agitation, it is like finding gold. I can use the answer over and over again, with similar results each time.

"If this stanks, Cody", I reply, "then that must be a good thing."

I let this sink in and monitor the quizzical look on Cody's face to make sure that my response has registered. "Because stanks is past tense, meaning that it used to stink, but it no longer does."

"Hunnh?" is generally Cody's response.

And while we continue our discussion of the appropriate usage of "stink," "stank," and "has stunk," we have continued with our exercise or the transfer activity, which initiated the agitation in the first place. In this way we can continue our work, while avoiding any escalation of the aggravation, and on most occasions, we can return to a joking and jovial session.

In this way, Cody's brain injury can be helpful. He is completely distractible. Like a pee-wee outfielder who can intently watch the game until a butterfly floats across his path, Cody can be taken off track by the slightest distraction. While this presents a significant challenge when Cody is trying to concentrate to learn a new skill, it sure comes in handy when I have ticked Cody off and need to redirect him.

"Where are we headin'?" asks Cody as we practice his walker ambulation.

"We are going to Iowa," I reply.

I have recently stumbled upon a helpful tidbit of information about Cody's grandmother, "G-ma". She refers to her couch as a davenport. Cody finds this dated terminology humorous. Add to it the fact there is a town in Iowa by the same name, and it strikes Cody as just plain hilarious.

"Where?" he asks with a chuckle.

"Iowa," I reply as we continue to practice Cody's stepping pattern, "on the way to Des Moines."

"Hunhh?" queries Cody.

"You know, the town not so far from Waterloo," I hint.

"Oh yeah," responds Cody, "You are talking about Davenport. I just love it. . . Are we there yet?"

"Not far now," I encourage Cody, as he continues with his three-point stepping pattern. We are just passing Peoria, Illinois. Can you name any other cities in Iowa?"

"I sure won't be knowin'," answers Cody.

"Well, there is Des Moines ... and Cedar Rapids ... and Sioux City," I slowly reply, expiring my reserves of geographical knowledge. "And here we are. We have arrived in Davenport."

We have just completed a walk of nearly 100 feet with hardly a complaint. Cody turns to sit on the davenport, thankful for having reached his destination. As Cody rests, I think about what will be our next distraction, as we continue our therapy session.

Cody was not always so agreeable to participate in physical therapy activities. As he has progressed physically, he also has progressed cognitively and emotionally. There were times early in our physical therapy sessions that Cody would become irate. Cody was especially fearful of his standing balance, and the physical therapy activities we were practicing were taking him out of his comfort zone. I am fairly certain that on more than one occasion, had his physical abilities allowed it, he would have hit me.

That was early in his therapy progression after his traumatic brain injury. Now, Cody is more able to control his anger, but he does occasionally become aggravated by my requests. Cody is most frequently bothered by positions that make him fearful, or in functional activities where he is forced to see his limitations. Recently, one of these challenges has been for Cody to stand and scoot a chair back from a table, in preparation to sit. This seems like a simple activity for most of us, but for Cody, it severely challenges his standing balance and forces him to shift his weight toward one side while reaching toward the opposite direction. Cody's control of his left leg musculature is limited, so it is difficult for him to control his stability when shifting toward that side.

Thus, when he is required to reach toward the right side in order to maneuver a chair, he will tend to lean toward that side, resulting in a balance displacement. My job as a physical therapist is to help Cody relearn these balance reactions. I help facilitate these weight-shifting patterns, but also, intermittently, I allow Cody to experience what happens when he does not shift his weight appropriately. Just as toddlers must experience occasional falls when standing so that they can develop the balance skills to progress toward ambulation, Cody needs to experience some balance issues, so that his body can respond to this input. His vestibular and neuromuscular system must reorganize, so that he can respond to balance challenges, in order to relearn to transfer and walk more skillfully.

55   55   55   55   55   55   55   55   55   55   55   55   55   55

At a recent Monday morning visit, I help support Cody as he sits on the floor with his legs outstretched. "Man, this hurts!" he exclaims.

"Where is the pain?" I ask, wanting to be sure the stretch is hitting the desired muscle groups. Cody points to the origin of his hamstring muscles. "In the hiney?" I query.

"Or the derriere," replies Cody.

"Or the patoot," I respond.

"How about the caboose?" says Cody.

"Or tuchus," I counter. After waiting a few beats, I continue, aware that I am asking for trouble. "Do you have any other colorful terms to describe your backside, Cody?"

With a grin, Cody responds, "I don't, but my mom sure does."

I ask Cody, "Does she talk like a sailor when I'm not around?"

"She does," Cody laughs.

"Does she use words like 'ahoy' and 'matey'?" I ask.

"And 'aargh'," replies Cody.

"That sounds more like a pirate," I say, "but I suppose that pirates are sailors too." We share a laugh continuing the stretch throughout the exchange.

§§ §§ §§ §§ §§ §§ §§ §§ §§ §§ §§ §§ §§ §§

Specific areas of progress for Cody have been in ambulation and transfer skills. As long as he has something sturdy that he can grasp, such as a grab bar in the bathroom, he can perform transfers from his wheelchair to another seat with fair control. Cody is challenged in stance by his left lower extremity tone. A result of his injury has been extensor muscles that no longer are well-controlled by the injured areas of Cody's brain. This makes it difficult for Cody to advance over his left side. His left pelvis tends to be retracted (or rotated back) as compared to his right, which results in compensations in his standing and walking pattern.

As long as Cody has the support of the side-rails on the treadmill, he is able to demonstrate fair, independent stability. He has advanced to ambulating for more than five minutes, with fair pattern, at a slow pace. At a recent visit, Cody was finishing his walk on the treadmill. "How many more steps do I have to take?" he groans.

In an effort to ease his complaints, I use the distraction of the Spanish language. "How do you say '50'? If 30 is treinte, is 50 cinquente?"

Confidently, Cody answers, "It's cinquenta."

"I think you just made that up," I reply.

"Nope, it's cinquenta," he assures me.

As we continue his walking pattern on the treadmill, Cody asks, "How many more steps do I have to take?"

"Cinquenta," I answer.

"How many's that?" asks Cody.

I laugh and respond, "I told you that you just made that up!"

Given these distractions, Cody is demonstrating an improved pattern on the treadmill. However, less skill is noted in ambulation within his anterior wheeled walker. Since the walker is not as stable as the treadmill, Cody lacks confidence when using it. Minimal assistance is required to help facilitate weight-shifting over the left leg. Verbal cues are needed to encourage Cody to advance his weight anteriorly, instead of leaning backward after stepping. In order to maintain hand-hold upon the walker, Cody must put forth increased effort. This results in an overflow of tonal influence through his left side, further challenging his stepping pattern over the left leg.

We are also practicing backward stepping activities with Cody. He has made some nice gains in this area. Cody consistently requires cueing to prevent a flexed posture within his walker. But, given these cues, he is moving posteriorly with fair skill. This is an important skill for Cody to develop, in order to assist his family in a variety of transfers.

"We need to get a beeper for you, Cody," I joke. "Just like the big trucks: beep, beep, beep, beep, so everyone knows to get out of the way."

"I just love it," chuckles Cody. "Can I sit down yet?"

"Well, we have a little further to go," I reply. "Your mom has left her wrap in this chair, and we wouldn't want to sit on it."

"We wouldn't?" Cody asks, looking for the closest location to have a seat.

"No," I respond, "that is a nice wrap. It is such a pretty brown color, just like a monk's robe."

"Hunhh?" ponders Cody.

"You know monks," I explain, "they're like religious brothers. Did you ever hear about the monks who live in Las Vegas?"

"Is this going to be funny?" asks Cody.

"Perhaps," I say, "it all depends upon your perspective. Now tuck in your hiney, when you bring that walker back. Anyways, these monks support their community by counting the chips for the various casinos in the town. Do you know what they call themselves?"

Certain that he has the answer, Cody can hardly contain himself. "Monk-counters!" he shouts with gusto.

We both share a good laugh. "Well, that is not what I was going for, but I like your answer better," I reply.

Cody thinks for a moment. "Or chip-monks!" Cody shouts enthusiastically.

We continue practicing Cody's backward stepping pattern. While taking a quick break, Cody calls for his mother. "Mommm! You have got to hear this."

Becky enters the room and asks, "What did I miss?"

"You are not going to believe this story," Cody says. "Jim, tell her."

I answer, "Cody, you'll do more justice to the story. Why don't you tell it?"

Cody thinks for a moment, then responds, "I can't remember."

And he can't remember, at all, what we were just speaking about. But, after a few cues, he gets the story going. I was right; it was better with Cody telling it. All the while, we continued to practice walking forward and back, in the walker.

55   55   55   55   55   55   55   55   55   55   55   55   55   55

Physical therapy for adults is usually fairly straightforward. Once you have the educational background and clinical experience, you are able to establish an appropriate plan of care. Each patient does present individual challenges in his or her presentation of symptoms and in their compliance with home programming. Yet, with patients who have undergone surgeries of the knee or hip, their post-operative rehabilitation plan is not particularly challenging.

Pediatric physical therapy is a whole different ball game. There is a certain knack to motivating children. Unlike adult rehabilitation, where one can establish an exercise routine and expect the adult to follow through, at least half-heartedly, children are not likely to perform a challenging exercise without some form of motivation. Anything that is perceived as work is usually met with resistance. So, the work has to be disguised with a whole lot of fun and distraction.

In therapy sessions, I will have children roll a ball down a flight of stairs to knock down bowling pins at the bottom, in order to practice stair climbing skills. I sing lots of silly songs; set up obstacle courses, and take turns in board games while practicing a new skill. Cody's physical therapy sessions are a combination of adult and pediatric rehabilitation. He cannot be treated like a child but definitely requires distraction with jokes, songs, or games to take his mind off of the hard work that is his therapy.

I help Cody "mosey" on over to the "swim up bar" (the name we have given the chin-up bar placed in the top of a hallway door). Today, no matter how much I try to distract Cody, I am faced with his agitation.

"Mom," shouts Cody, "how much are you paying this guy? … Well, let's just pay him so that he can leave!"

These outbursts are infrequent, and generally only occur when I have pushed Cody just a little too hard, physically. Another common, more pitiful plea is: "Mom, why am I such a 'tard?"

My typical response is: "Cody, you are not a 'tard' … a turd, maybe … but certainly not a 'tard."

I suspect that these outbursts occur more in PT than in any other therapy session, the reason being that Cody's physical limitations are more obvious to him than his fine motor or cognitive skills. As a junior on the Frontier baseball team, Cody batted fifth and played catcher for a team that advanced to the semi-state quarterfinals. Now, this once incredibly gifted athlete sits in a wheelchair as he laments. Between his sophomore and senior seasons of football, Cody amassed over 300 tackles; today he relies on my assistance to skillfully complete a roll from his stomach to his back. Whatever Cody's memories from his days of playing sports, he definitely senses how much his physical abilities have been impacted.

And yet, this same disparity that causes Cody some of this agitation also is a terrific boon. Cody remains endowed with some of his athletic abilities, which have allowed him to continue to make gross motor gains beyond a point where it is generally expected. My training taught me that the first six months following a traumatic brain injury typically is the period when a patient sees the most progress.

In the spring of 2010, Cody is approximately 3 ½ years post injury, and I have seen the greatest level of progress (since his initial rehab), over the past six months. I believe a part of that is due to Cody's past sports experience. Here is a young man who endured four years of grueling "two-a-day" football practices at the beginning of each season. Thus, 60 minutes of physical therapy activities are more tolerable for Cody, than for most patients. He knows how to work hard physically and is able to readily push himself to improve.

Additionally, while Cody does become frustrated by his inability to walk alone, he is highly motivated by the goal of doing so. Just as he was used to hearing a half-time pep talk in basketball, Cody is able to be motivated by encouragement from his family.

So we continue with these pep talks: "Mom, why do I have to do this stuff?" shouts Cody.

I had just woken Cody from a nap and was bearing the brunt of his agitation. After patiently waiting through the third blurting of this question, I take the opportunity to respond. "Cody, we're doing this so that you don't wind up on the Ivy Tech bathroom floor again."

Cody pauses from his tirade to consider my statement. The look on his face tells me that he does not recall this event.

"Do you remember that happening?" I ask. Cody shakes his head no, confirming my suspicions.

Earlier that spring, Cody, along with his mother, sister, and grandmother stopped to visit the Ivy Tech Community College campus in Indianapolis, following one of Cody's many doctor's appointments. His sister, Abbey, was looking into programs there.

While Abbey was speaking to the school counselor, Cody needed to use the restroom. It was a transfer that Cody and Becky perform flawlessly on multiple occasions each day. Like two experienced dance partners, they typically move skillfully, in sync with one another. Becky provides the support necessary for Cody to transition into stance. Then with this support, Cody is able to typically take a well-controlled step toward his target (a seat). However, this was not the case on that day.

Since it was spring break for the school, and no family restrooms were present, Becky found an empty men's restroom to assist Cody to the bathroom. Once she was sure that the restroom was not occupied, she entered the handicap accessible stall, and positioned Cody's wheelchair. However, in the transfer, Cody utilized excessive extensor tone through his left leg. This caused him to strongly shift his weight backward, resulting in a loss of balance for both Cody and Becky.

This is not altogether unusual, but typically Becky is able to help move Cody back to the chair from which he was transferring. In this bathroom stall, there was not room to easily place the wheelchair to complete the transfer. Rather than taking the chance of falling to the floor in a heap, while attempting to complete the transfer to the toilet, Becky chose to lower Cody to the floor in a controlled manner.

At this same time, Becky's mother was waiting in the car. She heard a knock on the vehicle's window. A uniformed security guard informed her that the car was in a loading zone and could not remain there. Despite her explanation as to why she was parked there, the security guard was unyielding, and insisted that she needed to move. He did suggest that she could return once it was time to help load Cody back into the car.

Back in the restroom, Cody lay with his legs askew. But Cody did not worry about the germs he might be encountering; nor did he worry about how long he might be stuck in this awkward situation. Rather, he did what seemed perfectly natural to him: He began to sing: "Jeremiah was a bull-frog. Doo-doo-do. He was a good friend of mine …"

On the verge of tears, Becky had to laugh. "If I didn't laugh, I knew I was going to cry. And what good would that have done us?" she later said.

After sharing a good laugh, Becky and Cody set about trying to get up from the bathroom floor. This was not the first time that Cody had needed assistance to get up from the ground, but they had never had to do it in such a tight surroundings, and typically Becky had someone else at home who could assist them. First, Becky attempted to raise Cody to the toilet, but this proved to be too challenging of a lift. So, she had Cody turn to try to crawl up into the wheelchair seat. But again, this proved too difficult for the limited space available. Becky contacted her mother on her cell phone, and heard of how the vehicle had to be moved. She told her mom that she was going to look for help, but to be prepared, if she called back, to come in to assist them.

Reluctantly, Becky left Cody, still singing, on the floor of the men's restroom, to get help. The halls were vacant. Having located no one else to assist her, Becky reluctantly contacted her mother again. With the extra help – along with a lot of hand-washing when they were done -- Cody was extracted from the floor.

After Becky retold this story to Cody, he laughed and joked, "Was I really lying on the floor of the restroom at some college? That had to be like totally bblechh!"

He made a face to signal his disgust. After hearing this story again, Cody worked diligently for the remainder of the session without complaint.

CHAPTER 8

CONCUSSION AWARENESS

After being inspired to write this story, I felt unsure about approaching the Lehe family. This was a very personal story, and one that I thought they might not want to share with others. I was pleasantly surprised by Becky's enthusiastic support: "Anything that we can do to keep something like this from happening to another family. I don't want to keep anyone from playing football. I only want athletes to realize when they have a concussion, and to be careful, so that they do not have to go through what Cody has."

What Becky is speaking about is education. Athletes, parents, and coaches need to be aware of the signs and symptoms of a concussion. This education is increasing gradually. Increased exposure through the NFL and other sports, has heightened people's awareness of the dangers surrounding concussions.

NASCAR requires baseline concussion testing for its drivers beginning in the 2014 season. The 2013 winter meetings for Major League Baseball led to plans to limit home plate collisions by 2015. This, in hopes of preventing increased incidence of concussions and other injuries to defenseless catchers.

In other, higher contact sports, protocols are in place. The Ultimate Fighting Championship has specific guidelines for its athletes to sit out for a period of 60 to 90 days following a concussion. The World Wrestling Entertainment also has specific guidelines related to ImPACT testing that must be cleared before an athlete exhibiting symptoms of a concussion can return to the ring.

This awareness in professional sports filters down to youth programs, as well. I am an assistant coach on my youngest son's U13 soccer team. In a game in the fall of 2013, a player struck his head on the ground after tripping over an opponent. Previously, we would have asked the player how he felt, cursorily checked his vision and asked him a few questions. On this day, we did those things but also decided to err on the side of caution and keep him out of the second half of the game. When this boy saw his doctor the next day, an ImPACT Test was completed. He was diagnosed with a concussion and sat out of soccer, and other activities, for two weeks, before gradually easing back into activities.

In cases like this, awareness is increasing and education is helping. In the past, if a player denied any headache symptoms we, as coaches, would have likely kept him in a close game. Furthermore, until the recent exposure of concussions, it is unlikely that his parents would have followed up with a physician.

The diagnosis of a concussion often relies on self-reporting by a player. This is frequently a challenge, as athletes typically want to get back into the game. While Cody did report his headache symptoms initially, he hid their persistence from his coaches and parents, so that he could play in the sectional game. This is where neurocognitive testing plays a dual role.

Previously, athletes would wait a chosen length of time after they no longer experienced symptoms. With the ImPACT Test, the athlete is allowed to return to action after meeting certain, pre-established criteria. One benefit is that each athlete gets to know the athletic trainer (or other medical professional) who administers the test and can feel comfortable approaching the trainer about an injury. Correspondingly, the trainer gets to know the athletes and can assess if their actions and reactions are appropriate after taking a hit.

The fundamental function of the ImPACT Test is to provide a baseline of mental function that can indicate a change due to injury. Upon reassessment after the injury, it can be determined when the athlete is safe to return to the sport, by comparing test scores to his/her baseline. The ImPACT Test is the first and most widely used computerized concussion evaluation system.

Five areas of cognitive skills are tested to establish this baseline and then are re-examined upon injury (or every two years to accommodate for brain development in young adults). The ImPACT Test is encouraged for all athletes over the age of 12. This brain function test assesses memory (visual and verbal), visual motor speed, reaction time, and impulse control.

The test uses a computer program to look at an athlete's patterns and responses. It is not something that an athlete can study for or even outwit. There are approximately 20 versions with patterns that change. It has been reported that some athletes have attempted to "dumb-down" their initial baseline to make it easier to reach, after injury. However, there are reportedly mechanisms built into the test to catch such attempts.

In regards to the goal of making sports safer, the ImPACT Test can help identify those athletes who may outwardly appear fine after a hit but have some cognitive changes. The test does take some of the subjectivity out of the athlete's return to action, and relies more upon data, than an athlete simply reporting how they are feeling.

As a proponent for the athlete, the test can help an athlete return more quickly to his/her sport. Previously, a concussed athlete may have had to wait two weeks after becoming symptom-free, but after producing normal results on their ImPACT Test, the athlete could possibly advance through a sport-specific return to activity more quickly.

When an injured athlete visits his office, Dr. Brian Morris, takes into account the athlete's typical grades in such subjects as English and Math -- as well as test-taking skills -- if no baseline had previously been set. He administers the ImPACT Test upon referral after an injury, then again once the athlete reports a lack of symptoms (such as no headache).

Morris typically follows-up in one to five days, as needed, until the baseline is reached. Without the ImPACT testing, Dr. Morris tends to be more cautious, since he lacks data from which to draw. If the ImPACT Test was in place at Frontier High School in the fall of 2006, Cody likely would not have been allowed to return to practice.

The return to baseline after a concussion varies greatly; all concussions (and athletes' reactions to them) are different and must be examined individually. However, on average, a professional athlete can return to activity more quickly than a college athlete and a college athlete more quickly than someone in high school.

Why the difference? It may be due to the maturity of the injured individual's brain. In professional athletes, the brain is no longer growing. A high school athlete's brain, while the same size as an adult's, is still developing. Thus, the younger brain appears more susceptible to injury, and, if injured, takes longer to recover.

Regardless, the treatment after a concussive event is the same: rest, eat properly, rest, hydrate, and get more rest. The brain requires nutrients to recover. These nutrients needed by the brain, can be depleted by a variety of activities. Television watching and texting, for example, are off limits for athletes serious about recovery. Additionally, Morris suggests reduced academic demands. Half-days of school with no test-taking is standard practice for those recovering from a concussion.

Research reinforces brain rest for injured athletes. A 2014 study in the journal <u>Pediatrics</u> looked at young athletes, age 8 to 23 years, who were recovering from a concussion. The researchers found that participants who reported the most mental activity took, on average, more than twice as long to recover than those reporting less cognitive activity. Limiting reading, online activities, texting, length of school days, and even homework can be helpful in speeding the recovery process. This study also found that minimizing mental activity – rather than excluding it altogether -- was adequate.[22] In effect there is no need to sit in a dark, quiet room to recover from a concussion, but a limit to mental activity is crucial.

Once the athlete is symptom-free, he/she will begin a progression to return to activity. The athlete will begin with light aerobic exercise, such as walking. Sport-specific training follows (such as throwing a football for quarterbacks or practicing routes for a receiver). Non-contact drills begin with advancement to contact drills, if the athlete remains symptom-free. This whole process can take days or weeks, depending upon the athlete's progress and symptoms (or lack thereof). If any symptoms are noted along the way, then the athlete rests for several days before beginning the progression again.

Yet, the ImPACT Test (or any other neurocognitive test) is not the absolute word in concussion management. In the assessment and progression following a concussion, the athlete as a whole needs to be considered. The ImPACT Test does present with some challenges for false positives. So, what is to be done with an athlete who no longer poses any symptoms (balance, headache, or other outward sign)? Should he or she still be held out of activity if their ImPACT testing still shows some concerns? This is where medical personnel's clinical experience comes in. Athletic trainers who know the athletes and physicians who interpret data can take a variety of information, including the athlete's report, ImPACT testing results, coordination/balance data, and other assessments into account, as an injured athlete prepares to return to his or her sport.

Neither a CT scan nor an MRI is a helpful tool in assessing a concussion. Cody underwent a CT scan, and it was normal. The only thing that would show up in one of these tests of a questionably concussed athlete would be a subdural hematoma. In a way, it was probably detrimental for Cody to have learned the results of his CT scan. Although the physician had correctly discouraged Cody from practicing or playing football if any symptoms persisted, once Cody heard that the results of his brain scan were normal, he felt like he was fine. In Cody's mind, it likely equated to an x-ray for a broken arm; as long as the CT scan did not show an injury, Cody likely felt that he had the green light to play.

The only imaging study that is currently useful for diagnosing a concussion is the functional MRI. This test shows blood flow-related responses to axonal firing, while the athlete is asked a series of questions. A healthy brain shows a stereotypical pattern of activity dispersed throughout its entire cortex, while a concussed brain shows an atypical pattern of activation when responding to the test questions.[23] This is currently a helpful research tool, but it is not cost-effective for broad usage. Other diagnostic studies, such as diffusion weighted imaging, which measures the health of axonal connections in the brain, may provide greater options in the near future.

Another test is currently being studied that may prove useful in the diagnosis and treatment of concussions. The U.S. Army has been studying a blood test that would identify brain trauma. The researchers have found that proteins spill into the blood from damaged tissue, due to the concussive event. These substances are not typically found in the blood of uninjured people.[24] Hopefully, soon blood tests can help to diagnose athletes, and others with concussions, so that they can be appropriately managed.

Researchers at Arizona State University, in an ongoing study performed in collaboration with helmet maker Riddell, compared blood and saliva testing with impact measurements from helmets. The researchers are looking at RNA biomarkers (a part of each person's genetic makeup) to see if there is a correlation between these concussive and sub-concussive injuries and the level of hits noted in practices and games. The goal of this research is determine at what level of contact, injuries become more likely. The Riddell "Sideline Response System" will measure the level of impact players receive and help to determine when to keep a player away from contact when this level is too high.[25]

Disturbingly, recent studies have found that it's not only big hits that result in brain trauma. The repetitive, smaller hits can be just as problematic. Dr. Ann McKee, associate director of neurology and pathology at Boston University, has been studying the brains of deceased football players. She has correlated a relationship between the repetitive trauma and significant, long-term brain damage.[26] McKee has noted that this long-term deterioration, while associated with the contact and repetitive hits, does not necessarily correspond to a history of concussions.

A 2010 research study at Purdue University, involving high school football players, demonstrated similar findings. Helmets of 23 players were fitted with accelerometers that measured the force of impacts, both single and cumulative. Baseline ImPACT testing and functional MRIs were performed for each player in the study. At midseason, 11 players took the ImPACT Test. Three had suffered concussions. The other eight were to serve as a control group for the study.

However, four of these eight players (with no history of concussion), showed significant declines in the visual memory portion of the ImPACT Test. In fact, those four athletes tested worse than their concussed counterparts. These four players had each taken a large number of substantial hits (40- to 80- G range) but not the concussive hits (80 G and above). Thus, the effects of head trauma appear cumulative from the smaller hit standpoint.[27] While it is typically the big hits in the games and practices that are checked out by the trainer on the sideline, it appears that the cumulative trauma may be just as significant.

Dr. Eric Nauman, Purdue University professor of mechanical engineering and expert in central nervous system trauma, is a member of the Purdue Neurotrauma Group, along with Dr. Larry Leverenz and Dr. Thomas Talavage. The group led the 2010 study and is conducting ongoing research in this area. Nauman states that the measurements of these sub-concussive impacts are significant. He reports that a culmination of impacts during one season totaling 700 Gs is significant. These athletes are nearly 100 percent likely to show some sort of decrease in cognitive function as tested on a functional MRI or in ImPACT testing. He further notes that those with a cumulative impact above 600 Gs were 60 percent likely to have negative changes in neurocognitive testing.[28]

A 2014 study also found similar results. Dr. Thomas McAllister and associates compared 40 NCAA Division I college football and hockey players to a similar number of athletes from non-contact sports.[29] The study found that athletes who play in these contact sports showed changes in their brains after the playing season, even if they did not suffer a concussion. This was not the case for the other, non-contact group. This concern regarding non-concussive events also is noted in a study led by Dr. Julian Bailes.[30] This study indicates that a concussion may not always be one major hit, but rather an accumulation of sub-concussive events that was the "last straw," so to speak. These studies demonstrate the importance of limiting the number of impacts that an athlete's head takes in any activity.

As the Purdue Neurotrauma Group has furthered its research, Dr. Talavage indicates that most athletes return to their baseline level of cognitive function as they rest in the off-season. However, he notes this return to a baseline is present "functionally. Non-functionally is an entirely different matter."[31] Talavage goes on to explain that the athletes that have been studied are returning to a normal level in regards to their results in cognitive testing, but upon the functional MRI, compensations are noted. Brain connections have had to change in order to allow the athlete to arrive at their responses. In other words, damage has occurred, but the plasticity of the brain allows it to circumvent these injuries.

CHAPTER 9

WHAT CAN BE DONE?

One of my favorite television commercials used to be for Snickers. It had the slogan "Not going anywhere for a while?" There were a whole series of funny episodes, where the main character made some sort of mistake or had a requirement that was going to take some time to remedy. So, he or she would turn to a Snickers bar to get them through.

One such episode revolved around a football quarterback. As the commercial begins, we see the quarterback take a big hit while being sacked. He appears to be fine, as the coach asks him a series of questions to determine if he can return to the game. The quarterback correctly identifies his location and recognizes the coach; however, when asked his own identity, the quarterback shows his confusion. In an overly-dramatic voice, the player responds, "I'm Batman." The commercial breaks to a scene of the chewy nougat, nuts, and caramel. When it returns to the football field, we see "Batman" take a seat on the bench beside a large, sweaty lineman. The quarterback states, "Hello good citizen. My name is Batman. Would you like to be my assistant?"

It does appear that the quarterback is "not going anywhere for a while." So, "grab a Snickers." As I said, this used to be one of my favorite commercials. It has lost some of its humor, since I met Cody. Needless to say, this ad has not aired since the NFL began to monitor concussions more closely.

Over 1 million young men play high school football in the United States. Approximately 63,000 of these are clinically diagnosed with a concussion each year.[32] There are indications that an equal number of concussions go unreported. This is of great concern, as those athletes who continue to play with neurological symptoms are at a greater risk for additional injury.

However, there is a new push for education regarding concussions. Where the previous, gladiator mentality resulted in players returning to games unsafely, there is now an awareness of the dangers surrounding concussions. As Bob Costas said on the September 19, 2010 half-time broadcast of NBC's Sunday Night Football, changing the football mindset is essential for the health of the players and of the NFL.[33] He went on to relate that caution has to be the key in handling a player with a head injury, and that medical science must be placed ahead of devotion to a team.

This has been noted recently in the NFL. In addition to new, controversial rules regarding fines for aggressive defensive hits -- especially those tackles leading with the helmet, there appears to be a larger role for the medical staffs of professional football teams. On November 7, 2010, one week after being taken from the field on a stretcher following a big hit, Indianapolis Colts' receiver Austin Collie was once again on the receiving end of several hard tackles. The cameras followed him to the sidelines, where he was examined by the Colts training staff. After ongoing discussions, a dejected Collie remained on the bench, while a trainer walked away carrying Collie's helmet (to ensure Collie remained out of the game).

The following month, Collie returned to the Colts line-up against the Jacksonville Jaguars and scored two touchdowns before suffering another head injury. When asked after the game about Collie's status, Colts head coach Jim Caldwell told Michael Marot of the Associated Press: "We lean totally upon those who are in charge (doctors). ... There's not a coach in the league who makes any decision based on anybody who has a concussion. Once he's cleared and ready to go, that's the case."[34]

After leaving two games with diagnosed concussions and a third with "concussion-like symptoms," Collie did not play the following week against Oakland -- or the remainder of the season. He did not return for the play-off game against the New York Jets, either.

In the 2013 season, Collie returned to professional football with the New England Patriots. He made several catches in the divisional championship game against the Denver Bronchos. It has taken Collie much effort to return to the NFL; some teams may have been leary of his recent history of injury and concussions.

Not only has this head injury awareness impacted the NFL, it has filtered down to the college, high school, and Little Gridiron ranks. Brent Fickle who coaches 10- and 11-year-old football players, notes an increased awareness in his program. The team's high school coach conducts an annual training for the youth football coaches. The youth coaches also complete an online training about concussions. In January of 2014, the Indiana Senate health committee passed a bill that would require high school and youth football coaches to take a training course every two years. If the bill passes, all coaches of Indiana High School Athletic Association (IHSAA) teams and those who use municipal fields would have to pass accredited courses regarding concussion awareness, player safety, equipment fitting, and proper technique for blocking and tackling.

A fall 2010 flyer from the Methodist Sports Medicine Staff in Indianapolis was sent to physicians, therapists, trainers, and coaches. It indicates that a priority is being placed on head-injury awareness. It is cleverly titled "Concussions Are Nothing to Play With." While advertising its sports medicine services, this flyer points out that a concussion without prompt and proper care may result in "decreased mental function that can affect grade point average and how one feels. If not treated properly and a repeat concussion occurs, there is potential for permanent brain damage and ongoing symptoms."[35]

In addition to education, equipment is another important area of progress. From improvements in football helmets to reinforcement of the consistent use of mouthpieces, football is ever-evolving in its attempts to keep its athletes safe. Currently helmets are designed to prevent cranial fractures, not concussions. Yet, advances are being made in this realm. Several groups are researching specifically engineered helmets to address concussion safety. In youth football, helmets can be re-certified every two years, in order to ensure their structural integrity and to replace any loose padding.

In soccer, headgear is an option for players to protect them when heading balls that can fly up to 75 miles an hour. My wife and I recently purchased headgear for our sons to wear in soccer practices and games. This headgear is made of the same material that lines the helmets of military personnel. The manufacturer's website indicates that its headgear is designed to protect the player's head from injury and impact. But the manufacturer was careful to delineate that their product is not designed to limit the chance of the player sustaining a concussion. No research has currently demonstrated any objective measures to substantiate this claim. However, after feeling the padding of the headgear, it seems that it would help disperse some of the force of a quick moving soccer ball. Regardless of the lack of concrete data, this protective wear gives my wife and me some peace of mind, when our sons take so many headers in games and practices.

In addition to efforts by parents, many high schools (administration and staff) are playing active roles in limiting the chances of an athlete sustaining a brain injury. Football programs are limiting the number of practices in pads, in order to help protect their players. This decreases the number of smaller, repetitive hits, and aids in the effort to keep athletes safe from concussions and other injuries. Ultimately, this helps the athletes to remain healthy to compete in games.

In 2012, the IHSAA made concussions a point of emphasis. Mike DeBoy, a high school football referee who was line judge for the 2013 Class 2A Indiana state football championship game, notes that the safety of the players has always been an emphasis. DeBoy states, "Concussion awareness has been a little more in the forefront over the past few years."

Officials are not just keeping players safe by throwing flags for illegal hits. "We really place an emphasis on prevention," says DeBoy. "It all begins with the coin toss. We try to set the tone for the game. We talk with the captains about playing a clean game and remind everyone not to lead with their heads when tackling. During the game, we might remind a player to keep their head up when tackling or tell a coach that Number 42 has been close to drawing a flag on a few occasions.

Coaches are usually pretty receptive to that. They don't want to see anyone get hurt, and they would rather be warned than receive a penalty. Preventative officiating can go a long way. Once we throw the flag, the hit has already happened. By then it is too late to keep someone from getting hurt."

Athletic trainers have noted this movement toward increased safety in concussion awareness. Corina Andersen, ATC, PTA, is an athletic trainer who has worked at many central Indiana football games. She has seen this trend toward a collaborative effort between coaches, trainers, and referees to monitor players on the field.

"It is so helpful to have the referees involved with player safety," says Andersen. "In smaller school settings, I may be the only athletic trainer present to assist both teams. So, to have the referees communicate with us, if they see a player struggling, is helpful. It is hard for me to keep an eye on 22 players at the same time. The referees are right there, on the field, involved in the plays. They have a good feel for how the players are doing physically.

Over the past several years, this role of the referees has evolved. They do not just enforce the rules of the game and throw flags. The refereeing unit is now an extension of the healthcare team, on the field."

On the sideline, Andersen watches the game from a different perspective. She monitors players' ankles, knees, and how a player lands after a block or tackle. If a player takes a big hit or acts dazed on the sideline, the athletic trainer will check the player out. As part of her assessment, Andersen checks the athlete's balance (asks to stand on one foot), memory (asks the day of the week), and vision (asks how much time is left on the scoreboard).

Andersen finds it helpful to know the athletes. "Some players are just plain goofy," she jokes. "They may not be able to tell you the date or recall three words (cat, purple, cow), even without a mild brain injury. If

I know the athlete, I will have a good understanding of their personality and can tell if they are acting abnormally."

To assess an athlete that appears disoriented, athletic trainers can have an assistant coach ask the player what his position does on a given play. Players are expected to know where to be on each play, so even if the athletic trainer does not know the athlete's personality, the coach can help to determine if there is disorientation.

If the player does not respond well to these assessments or he reports a headache, ringing in his ears, or blurred vision, Andersen will ask that he be cleared by a physician before allowing the athlete to return to the game. This is now Indiana law.

Andersen finds pros and cons with these new laws. It is helpful for parents and athletes to be required to take concussions seriously.

"Previously, I have had some resistance from both athletes and their parents when I have kept them out of an activity," she reports. "Now, there is no choice. The athlete has to see the doctor before they return to activity."

However, at times, Andersen says she feels the law takes some of her clinical training out of her hands.

"I have quite of bit of experience in monitoring athletes," she reports, "and these new laws do sometimes hamstring what I try to do."

Additionally, athletes may be less inclined to report to an athletic trainer.

"Players are no dummies," says Andersen. "They know the rules, too. They know that if they come to see me with concussion-related complaints, they will likely be sitting out, until they are cleared by a physician. Sometimes, the player might choose just not to report these symptoms."

To Andersen's point, in a 2012 study, high school football players filled out a questionnaire at the beginning of a summer camp. Researchers learned that while the majority had received education regarding concussion awareness, more than half believed it would be safe to play football with a concussion. Those athletes who answered questions indicating a better understanding of concussions displayed no better judgment in their decision-making than those less educated to the risks.

About half of these surveyed athletes indicated that they would not tell their coach if they experienced a concussion in a game. These football players felt that the welfare of the team was more important than their individual health.[36] The idea of letting down the team if an athlete chooses not to play, sounds eerily familiar to Cody's situation. This mindset does need to change.

Policies are evolving and changing in an effort to keep athletes safe. As research is expanding, so are new means of monitoring and protecting athletes from concussions. The information included here is as up-to- date as possible, as of March 2014. By the time someone reads Cody's story, research will have definitely evolved and the way of looking at concussions may have even changed. How concussions are controlled and managed over the next several years will play a major role in the future perception of the sport of football.

Despite the results of his injury, Cody and his family hold no grudges against the sport. This was evident during a post-holiday physical therapy session. While working on hip-extension exercises at the chin-up bar, Cody groans, "This stanks!"

"Well, it must be you that stanks," I reply, "because I got some cologne for Christmas. So, I know it must not be me, Mr. Fragante."

"What did you just call me?" chuckles Cody.

"You heard me, Mr. Fragante," I answer, as I help Cody continue with his hip extension exercises. "Fragante, as in fragrance, since you must have the fragrance of stank."

"Jim," responds Cody, "I love it. That is a funny one. How would you spell fragante?"

"Let's finish five more of these exercises, and I'll try to spell it," I counter. "Uno, dos, tres, cuatro, stinko."

"Stinko," says Cody as he takes a seat, "I just love it."

"Now fragante," I say, as Cody rests, "f-r-a-g-a-n-t-e."

"Do you know anything that rhymes with fragante?" asks Cody.

We have advanced from our facilitation of hip extension and are putting it into practical application as we prepare to do some walking on the treadmill. "Harry Belafonte," I reply.

And I begin a rendition of "Day-O." Cody joins in as I sing: "tally me bananas." Becky has entered the room and I am sure she is wondering how we got to "daylight come and me want to go home." But, to her credit she just watches as Cody continues his exercises and then she leaves the room without even shaking her head.

Later, as we are working on his walking pattern, Cody asks, still thinking of the name Fragante: "What is your favorite word that begins with the letter 'f?'"

"Fudge," I reply, thinking of all of the candy I have devoured over the past two weeks. "What is your favorite 'f' word?" I shutter as these words come out of my mouth. This could go horribly awry, I think to myself and hope that Becky is not listening.

Cody thinks for a minute. He has finished his walk. It was a very good walk, even after being less active over the past few weeks. He sits down and looks at me as he gives me his answer. "Football," he says, "that is my favorite word that begins with the letter 'f.'"

I smile. There is nothing else for either of us to say.

In review, concussions typically will resolve within a one- to two-week time-frame, if the athlete rests and progresses back slowly. In a small percentage of cases (10 to 20 percent), more time is needed to recover. If an athlete returns to activity too soon, he or she is more likely to suffer a similar or more serious head injury. Once an athlete has experienced a concussion, even when fully recovered, he or she is at greater risk of suffering another brain injury.

Further complicating the understanding of concussions is the recent research in the area of sub-concussive events. Not only can concussions impact cognitive function, but the culmination of minor injuries to the brain can be limiting, as well. These sub-concussive impacts may not lead to outward signs of balance impairments or headaches, but when added together, they have been found to lower athlete's cognitive abilities.

The takeaway point is the need to protect the human brain. This is especially important in youth, where the brain is still developing and thus more vulnerable. This is not a mandate for avoidance of such sports as football. Rather, it reinforces the importance of teaching athletes to play more intelligently. Displaying good sportsmanship, tackling with good technique, developing better equipment, and practicing smarter (with less contact) are all key components. Also, athletes must be knowledgeable and display respect for signs of a concussion.

Then, the athlete must act by reporting this information honestly and promptly to his or her coaches and medical staff. All too often mild injuries to the brain go unreported, exposing the person to much more serious injury, should another concussive (or even sub-concussive) event occur.

CHAPTER 10

CODY BEING CODY

In 2013, Cody was participating in some evaluative testing. He was asked to look at a picture and describe what he saw. Cody's father, Dale, was able to observe this session and later described what he saw in the picture of a park-like setting.

"I saw the general things. There was a lake, a house, a tree, and a car," relates Dale. "Cody on the other hand, began describing all sorts of things. Not only did he see the lake, he noted a boat with people in it. Cody described how both people were fishing, while one person was telling a joke. Cody saw two people having a picnic in the park. They were listening to music and drinking coffee. One of them was singing along to the music. His descriptions went on and on."

When the testing ended, the evaluator asked the Lehes if Cody had received good grades in school. "I told them he was an average student," says Becky. "He did just enough to get by."

The clinician went on to explain that Cody's responses were approximating someone with a near genius level of cognition. The Lehes laugh, remembering this conversation. "It figures," says Becky with a smile. "But we can never let Cody know that. He would never let us live that down."

Cody has developed into a truly unique individual. He has developed his personality and characteristics over his entire life experiences. Not only does the human brain take in sensory input from the eyes and send out motor responses to muscles for movement, the human brain develops to form a person's character. When the brain is injured, those who suffer from a traumatic brain injury often undergo a significant shift in personality. Additionally, humans learn from an early age to control and manage their behaviors. With a severe head injury, poor judgment, impulsiveness, and quickness to rage are frequently present.

Initially after the injury, this change in demeanor is seen to a greater degree, but judgment and demeanor can improve over time. Cody does exhibit some of these traits, but he can function fairly well in his interactions with others. His judgment can be questionable at times. It is not safe for Cody to remain home alone without someone nearby for supervision. Additionally, Cody can become overly agitated on occasion. But, in general, his outgoing personality and sense of humor shine through.

It appears that Cody was always a quite character. Dale recalls one occasion when Cody had to come out of an eighth grade football game with a cramp. On the sideline, the distracted coach continued to instruct his team, while massaging Cody's leg, in hopes of getting him back in the game. After a few minutes, when he had finished the massage, the coach looked at Cody expectantly, as he asked how his leg was doing.

Cody responded, "Well, that leg feels pretty good coach, but it was my other leg that was cramping."

In little league baseball, Cody enjoyed his position as catcher. He was good at managing the game and helping out the pitcher in tight spots. He would often walk out to the mound to help calm the pitcher's nerves. The pitcher and catcher would chat for a few moments. When Cody walked back to the plate, the pitcher would usually be chuckling.

"We figured Cody had a whole set of jokes that he told when he went out to the mound," says Dale. "We never asked what he said to his friends out there on the pitcher's mound. We figured it was better not to know."

"Cody, do you remember any of the jokes that you told to the pitchers?" I ask.

"I sure won't be remembering," Cody says with a laugh, "but I can tell ya they were all sorts of ornery!"

Cody is able to recall a portion of a story about his high school orneriness. Becky and Dale help fill in the gaps. It was shortly after Halloween, when Cody's Spanish teacher made the mistake of asking if anyone in the class would like to try out some of their new vocabulary words in a sentence. Cody immediately raised his hand.

When called upon, he exclaimed, "Senora Green es una bruja." (Mrs. Green is a witch.)

It did seem that Cody had learned his vocabulary words, but Mrs. Green did not find that to be sufficient. Cody was kicked out of class and was not allowed to return until he and his parents met with the principal.

Getting this glimpse of Cody's personal history, I learn that maybe Cody's personality hasn't changed that much, after all. Cody loves being around people. He can strike up a conversation with anyone, and because he is so comfortable being himself, he tends to put everyone else at ease. A lot was taken from Cody at that moment he was hit on October 24, 2006. But, he has been blessed with a number of gifts in return. One of those is sincerity. There are times when Cody becomes quite aggravated with me, but just as often, he tells me how much he appreciates my presence.

"Jim, you are a funny man. I just love it," he might say.

Or, "You are great. I sure love ya."

Or, "Wow, I sure should be sayin' thank ya."

Rarely do I receive such feedback from the children with whom I work. It is nice to receive such positive reinforcement, and the best part is that Cody means it whole-heartedly.

Another gift is Cody's magnetic personality. People cannot help but be drawn to him. My friend and therapy director at Cooperative School Services, Pama Schreeg has a heart of gold, but she would be the first to tell you that she is quite structured in how she manages her department and her patients. That does not work with Cody. Pama sees Cody weekly for occupational therapy services. And, I had to laugh out loud when I heard Cody describe an activity he performed with "P-shug," the previous day.

"Who?" I ask.

"P-shug," Cody replies nonchalantly.

As I have to do on occasion, I look to Becky for a translation. Becky rolls her eyes and chuckles, as she shares, "That's what he calls Pama."

"P-shug?" I laugh, "Cody I can't imagine anyone else giving Pama a rap name, and getting away with it."

"You're just jealous," replies Cody, "That you don't have a rap name." We all laugh, while I think that perhaps he is right.

55   55   55   55   55   55   55   55   55   55   55   55   55   55

During the summer of 2013, Cody was asked to man the registration book at a cousin's wedding. Obviously, this couple knew Cody well, as this was the perfect assignment for him. Yet, they didn't realize how good he would be at welcoming the guests to the church. The wedding had to be delayed a few minutes, as there was a log jam in the entryway to the chapel. People had gotten so busy visiting and talking that they were not being seated in a timely manner. The main conspirator in this was Cody.

As Becky described the scene at the church as guests were hurriedly seated, Cody just laughs. "And he is always so dog-gone happy," proclaims Becky. "Abbey and I were in foul moods this morning, on our way to a doctor's visit. After just five minutes of listening to Cody, we were joking and laughing right along with him."

As with most family errands, unless someone is around to keep an eye on him at home, Cody must tag along. "Mom had told Cody to zip it," says Abbey, describing her doctor's visit. "Sometimes Cody gets started talking and no one else can get a word in edge-wise. So, Cody was sitting quietly, for once, as the doctor walked in. It was my appointment, but Cody is the one in the wheelchair, so I think the doctor was just drawn to him. The doctor starts asking Cody questions, and of course they end up laughing. Finally, after what seemed like 10 minutes, my doctor finally looks over at me. Sheepishly, he says, 'So Abbey, I guess you are the reason we are here, after all'."

Abbey laughs and shakes her head. "And, that is what it is like whenever I go somewhere with Cody."

Becky jokes that traveling with Cody is like escorting someone who is campaigning for mayor. "He has never met someone that he does not want to talk to," Becky explains, with a smile. "Don't get me wrong, it is a good thing. But, sometimes I just want to zip in and zip out. This is not possible with Cody. I have to add a half an hour to the expected time for each trip. That is how long it will take Cody to visit with everyone along the way."

55 55 55 55 55 55 55 55 55 55 55 55 55 55

Periodically, our office will have university students spend several weeks for their clinical affiliations. Cody always enjoys when a student travels with me for his sessions. He enjoys having someone approximately his age to converse with, especially the ladies.

"What does she look like?' Cody asks, after I explain that beginning next week, I will have a student traveling with me for the next few months.

"Cody, I don't know," I reply. "I haven't met her yet. I do have some bad news for you, though."

"What's that?" he asks.

"I do know that she is married."

"Shucks!" is his response.

"That's all right, Cody," says his mother, "you can still be your charming self."

"I guess I sure can be," he replies. "What is her name?"

"Leslie," I answer.

"Leslie Altepeter," shouts Cody excitedly.

"That's right Cody," I laugh, rolling my eyes. "Leslie Altepeter. How did you know? Where in the world did you come up with that name?"

"I don't know," he responds, "Leslie just sounds like an Altepeter."

I smile, assuming that Leslie, unbeknownst to her, may have already been fitted with a nick-name before she even meets Cody.

One of my favorite things about Cody is that he is so very comfortable in his own skin. It does not matter who is present, or who they might be, if Cody feels the need to break into song, that is exactly what he will do. So, on that following Monday, I introduce Leslie to Cody. While we are performing some lower extremity stretching activities, I ask Cody if it is all right if Leslie does some range of motion activities with him, so that she can assess his muscle tone.

"No problemo," he replies.

As Leslie performs some leg movement activities, Cody begins to sing.

"Hey Mr. Tally Man, tally me bananas."

At this point Cody raises both hands to point his fingers at me, to let me know that I am responsible for the chorus. Now, in my defense, I had just met Leslie for the first time approximately 30 minutes earlier, when she arrived at our clinic to begin her affiliation. I am her clinical instructor and should maintain a modicum of dignity, at least during this first day together. All of this passes through my mind, but then I look at Cody's expectant face.

I belt out the chorus: "Daylight come and me want to go home." (Who says that Cody has a short-term memory issue? That is definitely not the case when it comes to music and singing. This is the song that we had sung the previous Thursday, after we concluded that "fragante" rhymes with Harry Belafonte.)

As we prepared to leave that day, Leslie told Cody that she would see him again in a week. As we walked toward the door, Cody offered her some advice: "Don't pray."

This seems to be an odd statement coming from Cody, so I ask, "What in the world are you talking about Cody?"

"Don't pray that the week goes too fast. I liked meeting you, but you don't need to hurry back," says Cody.

So, when weather cancelled most of the other schools in the area, Leslie and I had time to rearrange our schedules so that she could travel with me to Cody's home a day earlier than he expected.

"I guess your prayers weren't answered," I grinned as we greeted Cody at his home on Wednesday morning.

Becky chimed in, "You're always glad to see Jim come, aren't you Cody?"

Without missing a beat, Cody replied, "Not as glad as I am when I see him leave."

We all laugh. As always I am astounded by Cody's quick wit and his sense of humor. As Leslie begins some stretching and muscle re-education activities with Cody, he begins to sing.

"Don't a berry got no Mr. Roboto," Cody reinvents the song from Styx.

He holds out his hands expectantly waiting for Leslie to complete the chorus. Leslie looks quizzically in my direction. She had no way of knowing that she would need to expand her music repertoire for this clinical affiliation.

So, I jump in: "Domo ... domo."

Satisfied, Cody continues with the song. This time he begins the chorus singing: "Domo."

He waits for Leslie to take her cue. When she doesn't he says, "Give her."

Leslie shrugs and looks toward me, asking for an interpretation. I explain that "give her" is Cody's way of asking for the previous word to be repeated.

"Leslie just met you, Cody," I explain. "She doesn't speak 'Codese' yet."

"What did you say?" laughs Cody.

"Codese," I reply. "That's the special language that you converse in."

"Oh, I get it," responds Cody, "like Lebanese. Jim, I just love it."

55 55 55 55 55 55 55 55 55 55 55 55 55 55

Even with his injury, Cody remains a strong competitor. He will play some ball activities outdoors with me, as the weather allows. Nevertheless, Cody is not a big fan of these games. He will shoot a few baskets, but he does not relish the activity. Perhaps he doesn't like to be challenged by the sports in which he was once so talented.

However, when it comes to board games Cody enjoys the contest and very much likes to win. "Guess Who" is one of his favorites. (This is the game Cody and I were playing when I learned about David Hall and his lack of eyebrows.) In this two-person game, competitors take turns asking yes-or-no questions in order to eliminate possible candidates and eventually guess which character's card the opponent is holding.

"I think I may have played this game once," Leslie tells Cody, as we set up the game.

"That sounds good to me," Cody smiles, knowing that he may have an easy time defeating his new opponent. "I'll teach you how to play."

As Cody narrows down the options left on his side of the playing board, Leslie still has many characters remaining on her side.

"Is your person a girl?" "Is your person wearing glasses?" "Does your person have facial hair?" Eventually, Cody narrows it down to a last character. We explain to Leslie that she should make a wild guess from one of her final eight characters, because if Cody is correct, he will win the game, with his next turn.

"Is your person Nate?" she asks.

"O!" shouts Cody, as he stands at the counter working on his endurance and postural alignment.

"O-V!" he continues. Leslie sends me a quizzical look.

"O-V-A!" Some spit flies from Cody's mouth as he can't contain his excitement.

"It is OVA!" (over). And I catch a glimpse of the competitive fire that must have burned inside of Cody as he played high school sports. And, more importantly, I sense how much joy he derived from the competition.

Cody makes his guess correctly and extends some courtesy of what a good job Leslie did for the first time playing. He is hoping she will play him again, as he can sense that he can score another easy victory. I am glad to see him otherwise occupied, as he has stood for nearly five minutes while performing some dynamic reaching, without a single complaint.

55 55 55 55 55 55 55 55 55 55 55 55 55 55

Cody recently returned from a trip to a family wedding in Florida. Apparently, Homeland Security must view Cody as a major risk, as his mother says he is always questioned and searched. In their defense, the metal detector would not be effective in Cody's case, since he is unable to walk through the device. The metal detector probably would not be sensitive in picking up the difference between the metal wheelchair and whatever Cody may be carrying.

Nevertheless, it has to be stressful for Becky as she watches Cody being searched. One can never be quite sure what might come out of Cody's mouth at any given time. And, she is not allowed to be in the same area as Cody when he is being questioned. This time, she watched nearby while a security guard explained to Cody that he would be searching him.

It does, occasionally, take Cody time to process information during a conversation. For this reason, he has developed phrases that he uses to buy himself time until he can come up with an appropriate response. Currently, his favorite saying is: "You betcha ... I just love it." Typically this is an appropriate response in order to fill a void in most conversations. Occasionally, though, it just does not fit the situation.

As he sat in airport security, the guard told Cody that he would need to search him. Specifically, he indicated that he would be lifting up Cody's shirt and reaching into the upper portion of his buttocks.

The agent looked at Cody and asked if he understood. Right on cue, Cody responded: "You betcha ... I just love it."

As he listens to the story, Cody appears slightly embarrassed. (I didn't think it possible to embarrass Cody.) "Did I really say that?" he asks.

His mom nods. I laugh and to lighten the mood say, "My physical therapy visits don't look so bad anymore, do they, Cody?"

Cody laughs and responds, "Yeah, you might be a pain in my back side, but at least you aren't grabbing it."

55   55   55   55   55   55   55   55   55   55   55   55   55   55

Shortly after I arrive for another visit, Becky says: "I have to confess, Cody had a bad fall last week."

"What happened?" I ask Cody.

He turns to his mom and waits for her to fill in the gaps. "We were walking out to the garage and the front wheels of the walker caught on a rug. We tried to keep our balance, but the walker went forward on its front and Cody went after it. He hit his head really hard on the tile. I thought that he might have gotten knocked out, but he was soon acting fine and singing."

Knowing that Cody was all right, I joke: "Lucky for you Cody, you hit something hard like your head. You could have really gotten hurt."

"Yeah," Cody chuckles, "I could have gotten a really bad brain injury."

We all enjoy a laugh.

Becky continues: "I just had to know that he was doing OK, so I drove him to the ER and asked them to run some tests. Well, Cody had been singing: 'Hey, hey, you get offa my cloud' the whole way to the hospital. As he was being wheeled into the MRI, I heard him continue with this singing. When it came time to begin the procedure, I was asked to leave the room. From behind the closed door, I hear Cody sing: 'Hey, hey, you get offa my … ' I knew he was waiting for the technician to respond and complete the verse. Then, in a very uncertain voice, I hear the good-hearted soul sing 'cloud.' Satisfied Cody continued with the next verse of the song.

When the technician came out she smiled at me, and said: 'I think your son is doing OK. I don't know many people who could sing that whole Rolling Stones' song.'"

55   55   55   55   55   55   55   55   55   55   55   55   55   55

Other than an occasional family trip to Florida, Cody does not get to travel often. The narrow aisles of the airplane make it a significant challenge to help him transfer into the small airline seats. On another occasion, Cody was able to spend a night in a casino hotel in northwest Indiana. However, while Cody enjoyed the people watching, the room presented some accessibility issues. The whole family ended up having to move to a different room that was more suited to Cody's needs for transferring. Wheelchair accessibility and transfer challenges make traveling difficult.

With only these few trips since his injury, Cody was fair game when his sister suggested a trip to visit their uncle's fiancée in Champaign, Illinois. Even though it was a "shopping trip" with three women, Cody welcomed the short escape.

Upon my next visit, however, I learned that Cody's shopping patience had expired before that of his travel companions. Becky shared that as she shopped, Cody had eased his wheelchair toward the exit of the store several times, only to be escorted back by his mother. Finally, after being re-directed again, Cody gave up on his escape plan. So, he settled for another form of amusement. Cody located a sales person with whom to converse.

Becky shared that she was in fact watching Cody the whole time to insure he was safe, so she saw how the whole episode went down. She saw the sales girl laugh and say, "I couldn't possibly do that. That would embarrass me."

Becky could only wonder what Cody was up to and was about to intervene, for the clerk's sake, when she heard the young lady shout: "Hey Reba!" Reba is one of Cody's nicknames for his mother, from her full name, Rebecca.

Becky walked over to a grinning Cody and a nervous sales associate.

"I'm sorry," said the sales person, "Your son told me that was your name, and that he was trying to get your attention."

Becky assured the young lady that it was fine. As his mother pushed him out of the store, Cody chuckled, as he finally got his way.

It was the weekend before St. Patrick's Day, so the quartet of shoppers decided to stop at The Tilted Kilt for lunch. To Cody's pleasant surprise, the establishment was a pub that employed waitresses dressed in short skirts and generously unbuttoned blouses. The other members of his party were not as pleased with the setting, but they decided to stay anyway. Becky ordered a beer, and before anyone could say no, Cody chimed in: "I'll have one too." He had recently celebrated his 21st birthday, after all.

Cody enjoyed his meal, his beer, and his surroundings. Afterward, Cody's family asked the waitress if they could take her picture with Cody. She agreed and brought several of her wait staff friends over to join her.

After the story, Becky pulls up the picture on her phone. I could not help but laugh at the "fox who ate the hen" look on Cody's face.

"So, Cody," I ask, "did you enjoy your trip?"

He looks at the picture, to help refresh his memory, chuckles, and exclaims, "Oh yeah!"

Cody had enjoyed this bit of normalcy away from his routine of therapies and his altered, brain-injured existence.

CHAPTER 11

FAITH

On Sunday morning, Cody's father pushes him down the aisle at Blessed Sacrament Catholic Church in West Lafayette. In front of him, one by one, others bow their heads then extend their hands, in reverence, to receive Holy Communion. As Cody reaches the front of the church, Father Buckles smiles as he looks up. Cody extends his hand, with knuckles forward, and the priest bumps fists with the young man, before presenting him with communion. Surprised and somewhat embarrassed, Becky chuckles as she walks behind her son to the back of the church where Cody can remain seated in his wheelchair.

Some may find Cody's knuckle bump irreverent, but given his situation it is appropriate. Cody's faith has gotten him this far, and like all parts of his new life, Cody has made his faith his own. Cody was raised in a strong Catholic family. He went through First Communion at Blessed Sacrament in the second grade. He attended CCD (religious education classes) throughout his grade school years and was confirmed when he was in the tenth grade. Cody's memory of his religious upbringing remains intact to a degree, but bits and pieces remain fuzzy, as with many parts of his past.

To look at Cody's room, it is immediately noticeable that many areas of his life are represented. There are footballs on the book shelf. One is from the winning season as a junior at Frontier High School. Others bear get well wishes from Joe Tiller, retired Purdue University football coach, and Drew Brees, former Purdue great and Super Bowl winning quarterback. Pictures on the wall show Cody posing with friends. There is a picture of Cody, with two friends, dressed as girls for a football pep rally. There are pictures of Cody with his girlfriend at prom, and pictures of the semi-state quarter-finalist baseball team from 2006. And, then there are the religious images. Rosaries hang from a hook on one wall. A cross is placed directly over Cody's bed, and statues of angels peer over Cody's bed from a shelf on the opposite side of the room.

The many prayers of the White County community helped to bolster the Lehe family during the early days following Cody's accident. This email letter that was sent out to family and friends on November 23, 2006, shows how strong the Lehe family's faith remained during this challenging time:

> "Dale and I (Becky) want to wish you all a very blessed and happy Thanksgiving. We are extremely thankful for every single prayer that has been said for us. The prayers have been a key to Cody's recovery and have helped keep us strong and positive. Without all of you, we don't know where we would be. We are also so thankful for all the food, gifts, and monetary donations that have been made. We are thankful for all that God has given to us. The group of doctors, nurses, and respiratory therapists have been excellent. . . We will all be together this Thanksgiving in Cody's room at the hospital, praying for him and the rest of our family and friends.
>
> God Bless and Love to All,
> Dale and Becky"

Faith remains a focal point in Cody's progress. Recently, I read an article in the local newspaper about a trial for a drunk driver. The defendant had run two red lights and struck a young lady who was on her way to pick up her younger brother from work. The young lady had died in the accident. The reporter had interviewed the girl's father, who was glad that the defendant had received a stiff prison sentence, but felt no relief, as nothing could bring his daughter back.

In the same situation, I don't know that I could ever forgive a person who, through selfishness, had taken the life of someone I love. But, that is just what the Lehes have been able to do. While Cody did not lose his life, he did lose the life that was blossoming in front of him. As a senior in high school, Cody was enjoying a successful senior football season, and he was looking forward to more success in basketball and baseball. He had a beautiful girlfriend, whom he had dated for most of his high school years. Cody was a good-looking and successful student. He had every expectation of a wonderful future. His injury took this away from him, and from his family.

The hopes and dreams that the Lehes had for their son did not die with the accident on that day in October, 2006. But, those dreams underwent a dramatic change. And, while the family in the newspaper article was unable to forgive the man who had killed their daughter, the Lehes have come to terms with the sport that took the life that their son had enjoyed.

The Lehes love the Indianapolis Colts. Their son Zach has gotten to know Jeff Saturday, the former Indianapolis Colts center, through an organization that Saturday sponsors. And Zach continued to play football for the Frontier Falcons, throughout his high school career. The Lehes passed the practice field where Cody was injured 4 to 5 times each season, while walking to the stands to watch their youngest son play for the Falcon football team. While the Lehes may not have fully forgiven the game, they have come to peace with it.

55   55   55   55   55   55   55   55   55   55   55   55   55   55

Dale is a kind, patient man who works hard on the family farm. He, along with his two brothers, farms nearly 4,000 acres of land. Various wives, sons, daughters, nephews, and other family members pitch in when needed. The Lehes grow popcorn, dent corn, and soybeans. They also raise cattle, hogs, and a few goats. Their cattle operation is fairly substantial, consisting of 45 to 50 head. They also raise nearly 3,500 hogs each year. The Lehe homestead is a 100-year-old white structure, which has been updated several times. There are a number of grain bins, and nine out-buildings to house the cattle, pigs, tractors, semi trucks, and equipment that keep this large operation running.

Thus, Cody's home is the hub of activity, with people in and out of the farm, throughout the day. Most stop in to say hello to Cody, who always has a gregarious greeting for them. With his work day centered at the Lehe home, Dale is able to pop in frequently to check on Cody.

"Hey son," Dale greets Cody with a hug. "You working hard with Jim today?"

Cody shouts loudly with excitement upon seeing his father, "P ... O ... P ... S!" They exchange one of Cody's intricate handshakes. There is a lot of love between the two.

But during most of my visits, Becky is Cody's primary caregiver. Becky has worked a variety of jobs, including floral designer, wedding planner, and teacher's aide, in addition to helping out on the farm. But, her full-time job is being a mother to her children. Since Cody's head injury, that job has required overtime.

Nevertheless, the Lehe family does not appear to hold any resentment toward Cody's injury. In all my many visits, I have only seen patience for Cody. It would have been easy for Zach and Abbey to hold a grudge against their older brother and his situation. For nearly two years, the time they were able to spend with their mother was minimal, as she had to spend so much time away to manage Cody's rehab. Yet, the siblings understand Cody's needs.

Only recently has Cody been allowed to stay in the house alone for brief periods, while someone works outside and checks in periodically. At these times, Cody enjoys his freedom. He lounges in his Lazy-boy recliner, with a phone nearby, in case he needs assistance. Prior to this, someone needed to stay with Cody at all times to help keep him safe. On occasion, this responsibility fell to his brother or sister.

Both Abbey and Zach have had to put off doing things with their friends to "sit" with their older brother. The two younger Lehe children could have been angry with Cody for putting these demands upon their time or been short with him when answering his constantly repeated questions. But I have not seen this.

Instead, I have witnessed love. From the tender, patient care from Abbey, to the gentle chiding from Zach, their affection for Cody shines through. Abbey has even left encouraging notes for Cody. These notes go a long way in Cody's case, as words are quickly lost for him. Recently, I saw one such sticky note next to Cody's easy chair. It read: "Cody, I am sure proud of how hard you work each day. Remember how much I love you! (signed) Abbey."

This love is not a one-way street. Cody has a protective streak when it comes to his little sister, even though he calls her "Abb the Scab." And, Cody doesn't let Zach feel left out on this love, either. Cody provides the youngest Lehe with the typical teasing that only an older brother can provide.

"Where is he?" Cody asks, on a recent visit.

"Where's who?" I reply.

"You know, the stickle," responds Cody.

"The who?" I counter.

"The little stickle. Where is he?" Cody asks again.

Just then, Zach enters the kitchen, accompanied by shouts from Cody. "There he is. There is the little stickle."

Confused, I turn to Zach with a questioning look. "Don't ask," Zach replies with his head down. He quickly exits on his way to feed the cattle.

Innocently, I think that Cody is saying sickle, as in popsicle. Maybe it is a nickname shortened from Zach-sicle. So, I ask, "Why are you calling him 'sickle?'"

"Oh," says Cody with a grin, "I am not calling him 'sickle.' His nick-name is 'sticle', like testicle. … Ya' know … Uh-huh." With that, Cody laughs like the typical older brother that he is.

55   55   55   55   55   55   55   55   55   55   55   55   55   55

In a December 29, 2010, <u>USA Today</u> article, Vicki Michaelis describes Kevin Pearce's head injury. Pearce was a snowboarder with Olympic aspirations, and he hoped one day to return to the sport in which he was hurt. For the time being, Pearce's doctors urged him to take caution, as even a mild blow to his head could be devastating. For his part, Pearce felt fortunate compared to some fellow rehab patients. He had regained his motor skills to the point that someday a return to competitive snowboarding might be a possibility. Yet, a part of Pearce felt "unlucky" because he was not yet able to return to the sport he loved.[37]

This conundrum of being both lucky and unlucky describes Cody's situation as well. Cody and his family are lucky that he survived the initial physical threat to his life. Fifty percent of those who suffer a blow resulting in Second-Impact Syndrome do not survive. Cody's parents feel blessed every day to have their eldest son in their lives.

Yet, that life comes at a price. As my wife, sons, and I cared for my father while he was in hospice, we struggled to continue with the day-to-day requirements of our lives. I was coaching Luke's soccer team and was helping coach his baseball team. Our older son, Evan, was busy with travel soccer. My wife, Lisa, and I both continued in our full-time jobs, and she was teaching 3 to 4 exercise classes a week at the YMCA. Life continued on, and we muddled through, while making sure that someone could meet all of Dad's needs.

Eventually, when my father required 24 hour care, Lisa and I took some time off of work and hired some caregivers to stay with him. Sleep came at a premium for me during that time. However, I knew that we were operating under a timeframe. The nurse had told us that from the time that hospice services began, my dad could live anywhere from three weeks to three months. By no means did I hope that my father's passing would come quickly, but I knew that we could struggle through it if we had an endpoint in sight. We knew that one day our lives would return to some semblance of normalcy.

This is not the case for Cody's family. While his mother does leave Cody alone for brief periods to work outdoors (leaving notes for Cody to help remind him where she is, in case he forgets), someone must be with Cody for safety, at all times. While the family has a walk-in shower, Cody must have someone with him to assist him with his bathing. Cody has made gains in his bed mobility, but he still requires assistance to position his legs when transferring into bed.

Cody does continue to make gains in his cognitive abilities and his motor skills, but it is now more than six years after his brain injury. It is likely that where Cody is now functionally, is where he will be in the future. Many demands are placed on Becky, Dale, and the entire Lehe family to care for Cody on a daily basis.

My two sons are 14 and 13 years old. I have high aspirations for both of my boys. I have no illusions of them playing any competitive sport beyond high school. I do, however, expect them both to excel in school and go on to graduate from college. Would I be disappointed if my sons did not go onto college? You bet I would.

I imagine that Dale and Becky had the same expectations for Cody. Additionally, Cody had received letters of interest from various small colleges for football and perhaps could have played college baseball. A lot of dreams were shattered by Cody's injury.

In her essay, "Welcome to Holland," Emily Perl Kingsley writes about a couple who had planned a trip to Italy. The husband and wife were looking forward to immersing themselves in the culture and architecture of the country. However, due to unforeseen circumstances, their flight was diverted to Holland, and they were unable to proceed to their Italian destination. The essay goes on to explain that the travelers could mourn their plight, or they could enjoy the "very special, lovely" things about Holland.[38] The trip to Italy is a metaphor for a normal child-birth and parenting experience, while the detour to Holland is the experience of raising a child with special needs.

Cody would be the first one to tell you that he is special. However, in his case, there was a life filled with expectations that changed completely. Cody had learned to ride a bike; he had driven in the game-winning run; he had gotten his driver's license; he had fallen in love, and he had made plans for the future. Suddenly that future had been altered, forever.

As a parent, I don't know which would be harder: seeing those dreams come to a crashing halt, or never having those hopes and aspirations in the first place.

I was going through a very challenging time in October 2010. My father had passed away in our home on a Thursday. The wake was on Sunday and the funeral on Monday. Figuring that I would do better staying busy, I returned to work on Tuesday. I worked through the day, but I called to cancel my final patient, as I lacked the energy to work with her.

My father had been on hospice services for approximately six weeks with respiratory challenges, related to congestive heart failure. Dad had been brave throughout and was ready to accept his death, after having lived for more than two years without my mother. He was managing with minimal hospice support until the week before his death. That is when he had begun struggling to catch his breath, even on nine liters of oxygen. He had become intermittently confused due to a lack of oxygen to his brain, and I was up frequently through the night to check on him. In the days before his death, he required morphine to help decrease his apprehension over his shortness of breath.

Waking every hour through the night had worn me out physically and emotionally. I needed sleep, but I was experiencing difficulty falling to sleep after my father's death. I did not want to be back at work, but I didn't want to be anywhere else, either.

I returned to my full day of school-based physical therapy on Wednesday. I can't say that I put much effort into my treatment sessions that day, but I muddled through. One week after my father's death, Lisa and I met with the lawyer regarding my father's estate. I was sad all over again. I was looking over paperwork that reminded me of my parents, and I was seeing the many areas that needed handled regarding their estate.

So, when I arrived at Cody's home after the remainder of my school visits that Thursday, I felt sad and listless. Becky and Dale had both attended my father's wake. Cody had been with them, but he did not come in because the receiving line had been busy. The Lehes had made a generous donation to St. Elizabeth Hospice in honor of my dad. I had sent them a thank you note, and also wanted to thank them personally.

My thank you note had arrived in the mail earlier that day, so Becky gets it out to show to Cody. She reminds her son that my father had passed away the previous week.

"I'll sure be feelin' awfully sorry," he says.

"Thank you, Cody," I reply, "And, thanks for coming to my dad's viewing. That meant a lot to me and my family."

Cody reads my thank-you note in silence. "Who is 'Ho Spice'?" he asks after some consideration.

After a moment of reflection and confusion, I realize that Cody had misinterpreted my penmanship. When I had written the word hospice, I must have left a space between the "o" and the "s," leading Cody to the conclusion that the word was "ho spice." I laugh and laugh. Becky couldn't help but chuckle. Cody did too, though he was not sure what we were laughing about.

"Surely you remember the other member of the Spice Girls, Cody," I laugh. "There was Sporty Spice, Posh Spice, and Ho Spice."

Cody replies, "She does sound like an interesting character."

We all laugh again, and for the first time since my father began his significant health decline, I feel something besides sadness. I had almost cancelled my visit with Cody, but now was so glad that I had come. Cody has a way of instilling encouragement in every life he touches.

In the Lehes' foyer sits a chair that Cody uses when his mom gets his wheelchair. From there he can be assisted up the small steps into the home or to the garage for a transfer to the car. On that chair sits a brown pillow with the word "Faith" stitched on it.

One day while we were practicing stair climbing, I move this pillow and say, "Cody, help me to remember where I put this pillow. I wouldn't want you to lose faith."

Cody chuckles and responds, "You know you won't hafta be worryin' about that."

I smile, knowing that he is right.

CHAPTER 12

THE CONCLUSION BUT NOT THE END

A stand of approximately 40 white pine trees had served as a wind block at the Lehe home for nearly 80 years. The trees, planted by Dale's grandfather, protected the family farmstead and house from the strong westerly winds. However, a few years ago, bag worms infested the pines, and all the trees were lost. It was hard for the Lehes to cut down the trees. It signaled the end of living things planted by the family so many years earlier -- and the loss of a block from strong winds that could batter the house.

The side yard sat empty, aside from the many pine stumps, throughout the winter months. But once spring arrived, Dale removed the roots and cleared the land for the planting of small saplings. These 2-foot- tall white pines will not provide a wind-block for some time, but they do provide a hope for the future. These 40-plus trees will someday provide the same protection as the old pines did.

Just as the Lehes had to start over with these pine trees, so has Cody started over. Life at the Lehes' home will never be like it was before the autumn of 2006. However, hope remains. Cody will never play competitive sports again, but he loves to compete in a good board game. While running to participate in a sport may not be a future goal for Cody, walking short distances with a walker remains a motivating prospect. It was thought that Cody might not be able to learn to read or write again, but he has surpassed these goals and has advanced to complex thoughts and word problems.

And there is hope for future advances. Cody has participated in various experimental treatments in an effort to help improve his brain function. In 2011, Cody underwent hyperbaric oxygen treatments. The thought was that the oxygen-infused chamber could help repair the damaged areas of Cody's brain. The benefits of the hyperbaric treatments were difficult to measure, but Becky noticed improved endurance and fewer occasions of Cody "being stuck in the freeze." Such advances in the treatment of brain injury hold hope for Cody's future.

"If there is a chance it might work," says Becky, "we owe it to Cody to give it a try." Additionally, Cody's athletic background and his motivation for competition give him an advantage in continuing to fight for his gains.

Five years ago, one of Cody's neurologists commented that Cody would never be able to hold a job or finish high school. He went on to tell Cody's family about all of the things that Cody would not be able to do. This physician may be correct in regards to some of these quality-of-life issues. However, Cody has already proven him wrong through his accomplishments in many other areas.

While Cody may not be able to work in an unsupervised position, currently, his family is working with Purdue University to help find chores and activities for Cody to complete on the family farm. And, most importantly, Cody's contribution to the Lehe family and Brookston community cannot be underestimated. His sense of humor and complete appreciation of others is unparalleled. Becky has described how Cody "held court," whenever he went to watch Zach's baseball games. When the weather was too cold for Cody to leave the comfort of the family vehicle, Cody would shout to passers-by. As Frontier fans passed the truck on the way to the stands, Cody would converse with every person, and leave each one walking on with a smile.

This story is not the first time that the tale of Cody Lehe has been told. He has been the subject of a case study in the <u>Journal of</u>

<u>Neurosurgery: Pediatrics</u>, he was interviewed for a special on concussions on ESPN Canada, and his story has appeared in numerous online reports, including NBC News and ABC News. The Lehes have always been open to share Cody's cautionary tale. They hope to raise awareness and prevent such injuries for other young athletes. After the airing of one such story, Dale received a phone call from a gentleman from the state of Washington.

Dale enjoyed speaking with the man, whose son had also experienced an injury related to Second-Impact Syndrome. However, Dale relates how the conversation took an unexpected twist. The father began discussing their lawsuit. The family had sued the school system for allowing their son to return to play football, and won. The man went on to explain how the lawsuit had settled all of their medical bills and left them with adequate money for the ongoing care of their son. He encouraged the Lehes to consider such legal action.

I watch Dale as he describes the nearly year-old conversation, with renewed agitation. "That is why they call it an accident," says Dale. "No one wanted to see Cody get hurt. The coaches, the team, and the entire school could not have been more supportive through Cody's injury and rehabilitation. They were so good to us, and they acted this way because they cared about Cody. It was certainly not because they were afraid that we might sue them." Shaking his head, Dale adds, "I guess that is just the difference between people."

And I agree. My respect for the Lehes continues to grow.

55   55   55   55   55   55   55   55   55   55   55   55   55   55

Becky shared a story with me about a recent occasion when Zach called home. Cody answered the phone, and Zach asked Cody if he could speak to their mother. Cody responded that she was not there.

"Well, go get her," said Zach.

"I can't," was Cody's reply.

"Why not?" asked Zach.

"I can't walk," Cody responded simply.

"Well, why not?" asked Zach, curious as to what his brother might say.

"Because of this stupid football injury," replied Cody.

Becky recounts this story with misgivings. She was glad to see Cody begin to have some longer- term awareness of his situation. Cody's family has spoken frankly of his injury whenever he asked questions about why he could not perform certain activities. But, this was the first time Cody had discussed his injury without prompting. Becky relates that it was good for Cody to develop this awareness, yet at the same time, it was hard to see him struggle with the reality of the situation.

Just as the Lehes' wind block did not end when the first group of pine trees began to die, neither did Cody's hope for the future disappear on the football practice field on October 24, 2006. The path changed but continued onward.

Cody's story is an inspiration for me. We all face challenges in our lives. A person's character is determined by how he or she responds to these challenges. Cody has stood, with the support of his family, to face his challenges head-on.

During the time that I worked with Cody, I also helped to care for both of my parents during their hospice services. First, my mother battled colon cancer; then, my father suffered congestive heart failure. When I entered Cody's home for the first time, it was to help him make progress in his gross motor skills. Perhaps, I have done this in some small ways. But even more profound has been Cody's impact upon me.

Intimately watching Cody and his family face and overcome their daily struggles has been cathartic for me. When my mother died on the eve of a surprise birthday/celebration of life party that we had planned for her, I shared this information with Cody and his family. In my job, I work hard to keep professional boundaries. I always inquire about the families that I serve, but rarely do I share my personal information with them. Few of the families that I served knew of my parents' health struggles. I was more open with the Lehes, because I was seeking answers, and I knew they could understand. They helped me gain perspective from what they have experienced.

As I sat by my father's bedside on his final two days of life, I cancelled the rest of my physical therapy sessions. But, I kept my visit at Cody's home. I knew that I needed a positive outlet during this challenging time. I have provided physical therapy services for Cody, but he has provided me with mental health therapy. He has supplied me with much needed laughs when the days did not appear to hold any humor. Cody inspired hope and courage to face this challenging period in my life.

On May 26, 2011, I made my final physical therapy visit to Cody's home. I promised that I would stop to visit soon, and I have, for I could not pass up the opportunity to experience Cody's humor and unique perspectives on life. It was a sad day for me, because I had thoroughly enjoyed my twice-weekly visits over the previous three years. I thanked Cody for allowing me to share in his journey and gave him a small framed print that I painted for him. In large water-color letters, stood the word "Determination," and under this was a quote: "When the circumstances of life are grim, I will face the grimness, learn what it has to teach me, and walk on through."[39]

And Cody has faced these circumstances, head on, with a sense of determination and humor that are all his own. As I set out to write this story, I imagined Cody making such progress that I could write an inspirational conclusion. In the summer of 2011, Cody's uncle was getting married. Cody worked extra hard, so that he could walk down the aisle as a groomsman. That would make an exciting ending to this story, I thought.

Yet, it was not to be. Cody was pushed down the aisle in his wheelchair. However, his presence and participation in the ceremony were no less inspirational than if Cody had been able to walk to the front of the chapel. Cody's story does not have a fairy tale ending. Nevertheless, Cody is still in the process of creating his own story. Cody and his family live each and every day in the shadow of his brain injury. Cody, however, does not let this injury define him. In his story, Cody does not live happily ever after, but he does continue to live and enrich the lives of the people of the Brookston community.

As for football, Cody and his family hold no grudges. They enjoyed watching Zach finish his Frontier Falcon football career, and still cheer for the Indianapolis Colts. Since the time that I began recording details for Cody's story, there has been a movement toward concussion awareness and safety in all sports.

Over the past decade concussion awareness has grown exponentially. It has gone from a point where it was misunderstood and often ignored to a point where it is the forefront of many news stories and discussed in nearly every televised football game. Has the concern regarding concussions grown too large? Dr. Larry Leverenz, clinical professor of health and kinesiology at Purdue University and an expert in athletic training, thinks not.

"The pendulum has definitely swung in the direction of more elevated awareness," says Leverenz. "But, that is what needed to happen. Concussions are a big problem. We do not have all of the answers yet, but research is moving in the right direction. It may not be possible to take the risk completely out of sports such as football, but our goal is to reduce this risk to an acceptable level. Fans need to shout 'good block' or 'good tackle' instead of 'good hit.' It all begins with awareness."[40]

This awareness needs to continue to grow. Education is at the forefront of this awareness, and that is the reason that the Lehe family allowed me to share this information about their son. If one athlete, who reads this story, recognizes and reports his or her concussion symptoms to a family member, a coach, or an athletic trainer, then Cody's story will have achieved its goal.

Nothing can bring back all that was taken away from Cody on that football field in the fall of 2006. Yet Cody has been blessed with so many other gifts in return, including humor, sincerity, faith, friends, and family.

Thank you, Cody, for sharing these gifts with me.

Your friend,
Jim Cooley

EPILOGUE

It is now early 2014. Life has moved on for the Lehes. Cody has continued his outpatient physical therapy, but less frequently, due to limited insurance coverage. Currently, he is awaiting a new evaluation, in order to request a new authorization for services.

To supplement his physical therapy sessions, Cody has been attending a maintenance program through cardiac rehab at St. Elizabeth Franciscan Alliance. Most of his fellow participants are senior citizens, many of whom are recuperating from a cardiac bypass surgery or a heart attack. The 50-year age difference between Cody and his fellow exercisers does not affect him.

When Cody arrives, a gentleman greets him at the front door. The man wants to discuss the upcoming weekend of football games. Others greet Cody as he is wheeled past. The three ladies on the treadmill are granted a point of his forefinger and a "Hey, Babes!" as Cody moves on to his workout. The ladies giggle, noting that this is the only place that they get called "babe" anymore.

In the middle of Cody's workout, two older gentlemen join Cody in a handshaking demonstration.

"No you bump 'knucks' first," says Cody, trying to maintain his patience, as his students struggle with the intricacies of Cody's handshake.

"Knucks?" questions the gray-haired fellow.

"Ya' know," explains Cody, "knuckles."

"I sure hope I can remember this until next week," says the other gentleman.

And so on, as Becky describes how a 60-minute workout takes Cody an hour and a half. I laugh, knowing full well how this could happen. I also enjoy the story, as I am content to see how Cody has carved out a life for himself. Not many 25-year-olds would choose to socialize with octogenarians. While this is not the life that Cody had anticipated before his injury, Cody has made the best of his situation, and it appears that he truly does enjoy being Cody Lehe.

Cody hopes to increase his "face time" with his "peeps," as his mother opens a new business. After the past many years of caring for Cody, it is wonderful to see Becky find an opportunity for an outlet of her own. Of course, she would have it no other way than for that activity to include Cody.

"It was as if this business was destined to be," Becky explains excitedly.

She recently held the grand opening of her clothing and accessories store, called *B Boutique* (or as Cody has proclaimed it: "Rebecca Sue's Bou-Ti-Q"), in downtown Brookston. Cody will be able to go to work with Becky each day. He can hang out on the sales floor when he is interested. The shop has a back room that's furnished with a recliner and television for Cody to use when he needs a break. And there's an attached garage spacious enough for Cody's transfers to his wheelchair.

The Lehe family is still working out a schedule, but Dale is pitching in to pick up Cody in the late afternoons or evenings when he finishes in the field -- and Becky has found assistance -- so that she can still take Cody to his rehabilitation activities twice each week.

Becky notes, "I can take Cody to work and back home without ever having to set foot outside!"

I imagine Cody holding court in his mother's boutique as he has done at Frontier baseball games. I am certain that Cody's presence in the shop will enhance his mother's business. People will drop in just to share in some of Cody's contagious laughter, and others will linger and shop for longer periods, just to be entertained by this delightful young man.

Becky notes that Cody has been helpful in checking inventory. "When I get a new shipment of clothing," Becky explains, "Cody can count the number of red or blue blouses to make sure it matches with the packing list."

Cody smiles as he describes another role he has taken on. After noting a traffic-flow issue in the small space during the grand opening, Cody appointed himself "dressing room monitor."

"That sounds kind of creepy, Cody," I kid.

Cody replies with a disgusted but joking look, "Will you get your mind out of the gutter, Jim? I am helping to organize the ladies, not peek at them!"

And so, Cody eases into a new aspect of his life with vigor and enthusiasm.

Just as Cody's family trialed the hyperbaric oxygen therapy, Cody has recently completed a trial of Enbrel. This is a medication that is used in the treatment of rheumatoid and other types of arthritis. Sports fans may have seen this drug advertised by golfer Phil Mickelson. Mickelson has used the drug for treatment of psoriatic arthritis symptoms.

There have been recent studies regarding the use of Enbrel and its anti-inflammatory effects on neurological dysfunction (patients diagnosed with a CVA —cerebrovascular accident or stroke – and TBI). Becky indicates that an injection of the medication was placed between Cody's upper cervical vertebrae, then he was suspended briefly upside down. The medication is supposed to travel to areas of inflammation in Cody's brain, to help in his recovery process.

Since the treatment, Becky notes subtle improvements in Cody's awareness, and she finds that he is more involved in conversations. Recently, Cody was able to share with Becky new information in ways he never had previously.

"Hey," Cody spoke to his mother, "did I ever tell you that this is one of my favorite songs from high school."

Mild improvements have also been noted in Cody's use of his left hand. He shows increased awareness in his observations of the world and things around him. Recently, while watching a Colts game, the family was caught up in conversation. Cody gained everyone's attention when he noted that the clock had not started appropriately in the game. He was correct and eventually the error was noted by the officials.

Gains like these, though small, are huge for Cody as he battles for improvements in his everyday life. Though treatments like the Enbrel injections are expensive and results are not guaranteed, the Lehes note that they "can't not try."

"If there is a chance that some treatment can help Cody improve," explains Becky, "well, we can't put a price on that."

Neither can a price be put on an athlete's health. The goal of Cody's story is to educate young athletes about the importance of concussion awareness. Cody's warning to every athlete is: "If you ever have a headache (or other symptom) in a game (or practice), sit out 'bub,' right now or you are going to regret it!"

The Centers for Disease Control and Prevention lists the following concussion symptoms:

- Headache
- Confusion
- Nausea
- Dizziness
- Feeling foggy
- Sensitivity to light or noise
- Blurry vision
- Slowed reaction time
- Sleep problems[41]

If an athlete should experience any of these symptoms, or notes that he or she just doesn't feel quite right, it is important to get checked out. The athlete should notify parents, coaches, or athletic trainers. Continuing to play with these symptoms can make the symptoms worse, and, as in Cody's case, could lead to life-altering events.

Cody and his family want every athlete to be safe in his/her respective sport. They do not want anyone else to have to go through what they have experienced.

While he wants athletes to play it safe, Cody also has the following advice: "Life was meant to be lived, so live it."

You heard the man, get out there and live that life, just be careful with your brain when you do so!

READER'S GUIDE

1. The way that Cody has carved out a new, post-injury existence for himself is amazing. What part of Cody's story did you find particularly inspiring?

2. In the story, Cody states that his favorite "f"-word is football. In the year following Cody's injury, the family travelled to the RCA Dome to watch Zach play. How would you feel, in the Lehe's situation, about the sport of football that took away so much from your family?

3. Obviously, it is easy to second guess Cody's decision to practice, following his initial concussion. In the story, the author describes his poor decision regarding bumper sliding. In your youth, did you ever make a poor decision that could have led to severe consequences?

4. Given the many challenges that the Lehe family faced, it would have been easy to be angry with their situation and with God. How would your faith have withstood the Lehe's experience?

5. Football may face a challenging future, as participation in youth programs has recently decreased. NFL players such as Drew Brees have indicated that they will discourage their sons from playing the

sport, until their boys are older. What would you decide, if your young son expressed an interest in playing football?

6. Concussion awareness and education is the reason that this story was written. If you were speaking to high school athletes about concussions, what advice would you give them?

ABOUT THE AUTHOR

Jim Cooley is a pediatric physical therapist who has always enjoyed writing. He lives in Lafayette, Indiana, with his wife and two sons. The Cooley family enjoys hiking, biking, sports, and all sorts of outdoor activities.

BIBLIOGRAPHY

1 "Brain Injury Statistics." *Welcome to the Brain Injury Association of America*. Chicago Digital, 2014. Web. 23 Feb. 2014.

2 "Traumatic Brain Injury." *Centers for Disease Control and Prevention*. Centers for Disease Control and Prevention, 15 Aug. 2013. Web. 02 Mar. 2014.

3 Florio, M. "Aikman Opens Up About Why He Doesn't Talk About Concussions" www.profootball talk.nbc sports.com 9 Jan. 2011. Web. Mar. 2014.

4 Lombardi, Vince. "Football is Not a Contact Sport" www.aquotes.net/vince lomabardi/ vince-lombardi-football-is-not-a-contact-sport. Aug. 10, 2011.

5 *Sports-related Concussions in Youth Improving the Science, Changing the Culture*. Washington, D.C.: Natl Academy Pr, 2014. Print.

6 "Sports and Play, Concussions" *Centers for Disease Control and Prevention*. Centers for Disease Control and Prevention, 15 Aug. 2013. Web. 02 Mar. 2014.

7 *Sports-related Concussions in Youth Improving the Science, Changing the Culture*. Washington, D.C.: Natl Academy Pr, 2014. Print.

8 Mccrea, M. "Acute Effects and Recovery Time Following Concussion in Collegiate Football Players: The NCAA Concussion Study." *JAMA: The Journal of the American Medical Association* 290.19 (2003): 2556-563. Print.

9 Mckeag, D. B. "Understanding Sports-Related Concussion: Coming Into Focus but Still Fuzzy." *JAMA: The Journal of the American Medical Association* 290.19 (2003): 2604-605. Print.

[10] Harmon, K. G. "American Medical Society for Sports Medicine Position Statement: Concussion in Sport"" *Br J Sports Med* 47 (2013): 15-26. *Bjsm.bmj.com.* Web.

[11] *Sports-related Concussions in Youth Improving the Science, Changing the Culture.* Washington, D.C.: Natl Academy Pr, 2014. Print.

[12] "Sports and Play, Concussions" *Centers for Disease Control and Prevention.* Centers for Disease Control and Prevention, 15 Aug. 2013. Web. 02 Mar. 2014.

[13] Brees, Drew, and Chris Fabry. *Coming Back Stronger.* Carol Stream, IL: Tyndale House, 2010. 26% e reader.

[14] "Grades of Concussion" *Neurology* 48 (1997): 581-85. Web.

[15] Leverenz, Larry, Ph.D., Nauman, Eric, Ph.D, & Talavage, Thomas, Ph.D. "Interview With the Purdue Neurotrauma Group." Personal interview. 15 Jan. 2014.

[16] Eliason, J. M. "Second Impact Syndrome: A Devastating Injury to a Young Brain" *Journal of Neurosurgery: Pediatrics* (2013): n. pag. *Public Release.* Eureka Alert. Web.

[17] Moore, Josephine C., Ph.D., OTR, FAOTA, D.Sc. "The Neuroanatomy of Closed Head and Brain Injury in Children and Adults" www.clinicians-view.com. 1 Dec. 2013.

[18] Weissbluth, D. D. *"Lehe, Cody Discharge Summary"* Indianapolis, IN: Methodist Hospital, January, 31 2007. Print.

[19] Kisner, Carolyn, and Lynn Allen. Colby. *Therapeutic Exercise: Foundations and Techniques.* Philadelphia: F.A. Davis, 2007. Print.

[20] Ibid.

[21] Leverenz, Larry, Ph.D., Nauman, Eric, Ph.D, & Talavage, Thomas, Ph.D. "Interview With the Purdue Neurotrauma Group." Personal interview. 15 Jan. 2014.

[22] Brown, N. J., R. C. Mannix, and M. J. O'Brien. "Effect of Cognitive Activity Level on Duration of Post- Concussion Symptoms" *Pediatrics* (2014): 2125. *Pediatrics.aappublications.org.* Web. 8 Mar. 2014.

23 Leverenz, Larry, Ph.D., Nauman, Eric, Ph.D, & Talavage, Thomas, Ph.D. "Interview With the Purdue Neurotrauma Group." Personal interview. 15 Jan. 2014.

24 Lopez, C. T. "Army Looking at Blood Test for Concussions" *www.army.mil*. The United States Army, 13 May 2011. Web. 8 Mar. 2014.

25 Beck, I.C. "Partnering with Riddell in Concussion Study a Great Move for ASU Football." www.statepress.com, 18 Sept. 2013. Web. 8 Mar. 2014.

26 King, P. "Concussions (The Hits That Are Changing Football)" *Sports Illustrated* 1 Nov. 2010: *SI Vault*. Web. 3 Mar. 2013.

27 Talavage, T. M., E. Nauman, E. L. Breedlove, et al. "Functionally-Detected Cognitive Impairment in High School Football Players Without Clinically-Diagnosed Concussion" *Journal of Neurotrauma* (2011): 110306202455053. Print.

28 Leverenz, Larry, Ph.D., Nauman, Eric, Ph.D, & Talavage, Thomas, Ph.D. "Interview With the Purdue Neurotrauma Group." Personal interview. 15 Jan. 2014.

29 McAllister, T. W., J. C. Ford, L. A. Flashman, et al. "Effect of Head Impacts on Diffusivity Measures in a Cohort of Collegiate Contact Sports Athletes" *Neurology* 82 (2014): 1-7. Web.

30 Bailes, J. E., A. L. Petraglia, B. I. Omalu, et al. "Role of Subconcussion in Repetitive Mild Traumatic Brain Injury." *Journal of Neurosurgery* 119.5 (2013): 1235-245. Print.

31 Leverenz, Larry, Ph.D., Nauman, Eric, Ph.D, & Talavage, Thomas, Ph.D. "Interview With the Purdue Neurotrauma Group." Personal interview. 15 Jan. 2014.

32 Talavage, T. M., E. Nauman, E. L. Breedlove, et al. "Functionally-Detected Cognitive Impairment in High School Football Players Without Clinically-Diagnosed Concussion" *Journal of Neurotrauma* (2011): 110306202455053. Print.

33 Costas, Bob. "NFL Sunday Night Football." *"Football NightiIn America"* NBC. New York, New York, 19 Dec. 2010. Television. Transcript.

34   Marot, M. "Indianapolis Wide Receiver Collie's Status Unclear" *The Associated Press* [Lafayette Journal & Courier] 21 Dec. 2010: C3. Print.

35   Methodist Hospital Sports Medicine. *Concussions Are Nothing to Play With*. Indianapolis, IN: Methodist Hospital, 2010. Print.

36   B. Anderson et al. ""I Can't Miss the Big Game": High School (HS) Football Players' Knowledge and Attitudes About Concussions." Abstract #3165.4. Pediatric Academic Societies Annual Meeting, Washington, D.C. May 4-7, 2013.

37   Michaelis, V. "Year After Crash, Pearce Waits to Board" *USA Today* 29 Dec. 2010: 5C. Print.

38   Kingsley, Emily P. "Welcome to Holland" (1987): *www.ourkids.org/ archives/ Holland*. Web. 8 Mar. 2014.

39   Hickman, Martha Whitmore. *Healing after Loss: A Daily Journal for Working through Grief*. New York: Avon Books, 1994. Print.

40   Leverenz, Larry, Ph.D., Nauman, Eric, Ph.D, & Talavage, Thomas, Ph.D. "Interview With the Purdue Neurotrauma Group." Personal interview. 15 Jan. 2014.

41   "Sports and Play, Concussions" *Centers for Disease Control and Prevention*. Centers for Disease Control and Prevention, 15 Aug. 2013. Web. 02 Mar. 2014.

CPSIA information can be obtained at www.ICGtesting.com
Printed in the USA
BVOW07s2357220914

367914BV00001BA/55/P